In *Therapy with Troubled Teenagers,* Bob
Bertolino describes his unique approach to
treating adolescents and their families. He
applies possibility-oriented interventions that
focus on eliciting, evoking, and highlighting
the strengths of clients, as opposed to their
pathology and deficits. This approach, which
is collaborative, resource-focused, respectful,
and generally brief, is a highly effective type of
therapy for young people at this fragile stage of
life. Bertolino has collaborated with Bill
O'Hanlon—pioneer in solution-oriented and
possibility therapies, and the author of the
Foreword for this book—and has expanded
on and applied O'Hanlon's ideas to his work
with troubled youth, including juvenile
offenders and adolescents with substance-
abuse or behavioral problems, with positive
and successful results.

Bertolino begins the book by outlining the
four common factors that can facilitate
therapy and make a difference for both adolescents and their families. He discusses the
importance of *experience, stories, action,* and
context in therapy—the four different domains
that this type of approach to therapy
encompasses—and explains why effective
communication is absolutely crucial. The way
we talk about problems, solutions, and possibilities can greatly influence the direction of
therapy. Collaborative language is key because
it opens up pathways with endless possibilities
for young people who may feel that they have
no escape from their troubles. Bertolino also
offers invaluable advice on gaining a focus and
establishing goals in therapy, two steps that are
critical to making a difference. One of the last
stages of the process is getting the adolescents
to envision a future where things work out,
and then planning the steps for making that
vision a reality. The final part of the book
presents a comprehensive case study, which
illustrates the ideas and therapeutic principles
presented in the book.

D0407938

THERAPY WITH TROUBLED TEENAGERS

THERAPY WITH TROUBLED TEENAGERS

REWRITING YOUNG LIVES IN PROGRESS

Bob Bertolino

JOHN WILEY & SONS, INC.

New York • Chichester • Weinheim • Brisbane • Singapore • Toronto

View-Master® is a registered trademark of The Fisher-Price Corporation (East Eudora, NY).

This book is printed on acid-free paper. ∞

Copyright © 1999 by John Wiley & Sons, Inc. All rights reserved.

Published simultaneously in Canada.

No part of this publication may be reproduced, stored in a retrieval system or transmitted in any form or by any means, electronic, mechanical, photocopying, recording, scanning or otherwise, except as permitted under Sections 107 or 108 of the 1976 United States Copyright Act, without either the prior written permission of the Publisher, or authorization through payment of the appropriate per-copy fee to the Copyright Clearance Center, 222 Rosewood Drive, Danvers, MA 01923, (978) 750-8400, fax (978) 750-4744. Requests to the Publisher for permission should be addressed to the Permissions Department, John Wiley & Sons, Inc., 605 Third Avenue, New York, NY 10158-0012, (212) 850-6011, fax (212) 850-6008, E-Mail: PERMREQ@WILEY.COM.

This publication is designed to provide accurate and authoritative information in regard to the subject matter covered. It is sold with the understanding that the publisher is not engaged in rendering professional services. If professional advice or other expert assistance is required, the services of a competent professional person should be sought.

Library of Congress Cataloging-in-Publication Data:

Bertolino, Bob, 1965–
    Therapy with troubled teenagers : rewriting young lives in
progress / Bob Bertolino.
        p.   cm.
    Includes index.
    ISBN 0-471-24996-3 (cloth : alk. paper)
    1. Problem youth—Counseling of.   2. Adolescent psychotherapy.
3. Solution-focused therapy.   I. Title.
RJ506.P638475   1999
616.89' 14' 0835—dc21   98-9520

Printed in the United States of America.

10   9   8   7   6   5   4   3   2   1

To my wife, Christine,
for all the possibilities you have brought to my life.

CONCORDIA UNIVERSITY LIBRARY
PORTLAND, OR 97211

FOREWORD

*W*HEN I WAS A *teenager, I had dreams of becoming a rock star guitarist. In those days, the pinnacle was Jimi Hendrix. He seemed to be able to play anything he thought, instantly and masterfully. I knew that I would never be able to play like him, but I aspired to get as close as I could. So, imagine my dismay when, several years later, while walking down the street near the university I attended, I came across two teenagers who had set up guitars and amplifiers on a bench in a park, and were playing Jimi Hendrix guitar solos note for note. They had obviously mastered his style early in their musical careers and were ready to move on. I thought that rock would become even more interesting and challenging with these youngsters driving it in the future.*

Bob Bertolino has done something akin to that in this book. He has mastered the approaches of the premier contributors to respectful, collaborative therapies and put them into practice in innovative ways. I think the future of therapy, especially with difficult and challenging adolescents and their families, will be even more interesting and effective when approached from the base Bob Bertolino provides. This is a practical, immediately useful book for those working with difficult and challenging adolescents. The examples bring to life the clear and coherent theoretical frameworks. Much of the time, when I read such books, I disbelieve the case examples—both the details and the miraculous results reported. The examples in this book, though, strike me as dispatches from the front lines of real treatment. I recognize some of these kids and their families, and the dilemmas they face.

We therapists want to prevent "troubled" youth (and do you know any adolescent who isn't troubled in some way?) from becoming career "mental patients" or criminals. Unfortunately, sometimes we unwittingly contribute to that process by our approaches to these challenging and often hostile, uncommunicative, self-sabotaging kids.

I met Bob years ago, but I remember when he and I first really connected. We had corresponded a bit and spoken on the phone. He had come to some of my training sessions and seemed a bright and capable guy. Several years ago, I visited St. Louis, the area in which he lived, to teach a workshop. Bob offered to give me a ride to the airport after the workshop. Because we had a bit of time before my plane left, we decided to stop by his house to retrieve something he needed, and then to have a quick dinner before heading to the airport. At his house, I sat in his home office with his then-fiancée, now wife, Christine. His bookshelves were filled with every book and tape about collaborative, solution-based, narrative, and constructivist approaches to therapy, some of which I didn't own or hadn't read. Christine said that this was Bob's sanctuary, where he spent countless hours listening to or watching tapes, writing, and reading. She told me that Bob was obsessed with this material. At the time, Bob was working toward his doctorate, teaching part-time at a university, working full-time at an adolescent treatment center, and playing in an "alternative" rock and roll band several nights a week (the band made two CDs, comprised mostly of Bob's songs). I remarked to Christine that I used to be like that, in my younger and more energetic days. At dinner, Bob enthusiastically suggested that I write a book detailing my ideas for working with sexual abuse problems in a brief and respectful manner; he thought my material was very different from the methods and philosophies current in the field. I laughed and told him that I was busy this decade and had decided to stop writing for several years (after writing ten books in ten years). But on the way home, I thought more and more about the book project. When I arrived home, I immediately faxed Bob an outline and asked him to coauthor the book he had suggested. We found we worked together well. We not only finished that book (*Even From a Broken Web*, Wiley, 1998), but have gone on to collaborate on several other projects. He has finished two other books with me in the course of the past year, and he has coedited another one with my wife, Steffanie. During that same year, Bob finished his dissertation, got married, and finished the book you hold in your hands. I had occasion to speak to one of Bob's colleagues at the adolescent treatment center where he worked. She told me that, even worse, his case records were always done promptly and clearly. And to top it off, he happens to be a truly nice and easygoing guy. Isn't this disgusting?

What I am trying to say is that I think Bob has a bright future in the field of psychotherapy, and the field has a brighter future because we have him.

Bill O'Hanlon

Santa Fe, New Mexico

PREFACE

I do what I do with all my strength and heart.

—Lucille Ball

I look at you and I think that someday our humanity might actually surpass our technology.

—Jeff Goldblum, in the motion picture, *Powder*

A WOMAN BROUGHT HER *15-year-old son to therapy after he had been arrested for breaking and entering, and possession of a handgun. She described how he had been a "good kid" with passing grades and no run-ins with the law until he had reached 14 years of age. At that time, he began incrementally breaking curfew, running away from home, and stealing from local convenience stores and gas stations. This conduct was then surpassed by more serious charges. At the first session, the woman stated that she wanted to have her son placed in residential treatment. She felt that there was no hope of his changing. She said, "I've tried to teach him right from wrong. What else can I do? I feel like I've failed as a parent. But I don't think it's just me. Just look at these kids today. They do what they want, when they want, and they don't care about anything . . . . And some of them are so damn mean—what's going on here?"*

Does this sound familiar? Perhaps it's all too familiar! This woman's story about her son in today's world is not unusual. She was once a teenager too, but could not comprehend the behavior of her son. When she was young, had she slightly disobeyed her parents, the consequences would have been severe. That was enough to deter her from behaving poorly. Now, as a mother, she saw herself as inadequate, blamed, guilty, and a failure. She also felt hopeless and without options or recourse. To cause further distress, the unruly behavior she saw in her son was only a hint of what she had witnessed in other adolescents.

Since the late 1980s, through my work at Youth in Need, Inc., in St. Charles, Missouri, I have been educated and trained by some of the best teachers possible—adolescents and families such as the one just described. The teachings of my mentor, Bill O'Hanlon, also have been of great influence. This background has led to the journey that this book represents. You will be part of a collaborative effort informed by clients and clinicians, and a culmination of experience, practice, and theory—a *possibility therapy* approach to working with adolescents and families. But before we go any further, let's get an idea of what we are facing.

WHAT'S GOING ON HERE?

Although I sometimes use the term *troubled,* it is not intended to convey that something is personally or characteristically wrong with a youth. I am merely describing those adolescents between the ages of 10 and 18 years who have exhibited problematic behavior—for example, fighting with siblings, failing classes in school, or refusing to follow rules at home. On other occasions, the trouble is more severe and includes bouts with status, misdemeanor, and felony offenses.

Status offenses are behaviors that are unlawful for youth, even though they are legal for adults. They generally include curfew violation, truancy, running away from home, alcohol possession, and incorrigibility (disobedience). Misdemeanor and felony offenses can include, but are not limited to, assault, breaking and entering, theft, distribution of narcotics, and possession of weapons. Many adolescents who are experiencing trouble are labeled as "bad" and are considered unchangeable. Many also become "throwaways"; their parents or guardians give up on them and, in some instances, cast them out of their lives. Members of society frequently stereotype adolescents in these predicaments as future criminals.

The media, through research statistics and crime stories, often paint a dim picture of youth who have had or are experiencing trouble. For example, a Fox News poll recently found that 37% of American adults were greatly concerned about how the youth of today might run the country in the future (June 26, 1997).

Statistical research paints an even grimmer picture. The number of adolescents who are experiencing severe problems with the law is on the rise. In fact, in 1995 police made 2.7 million arrests of juveniles nationally (Federal Bureau of Investigation, 1996). Ironically, this data represented only the cases that were processed! Snyder (1996) remarked, "Almost all juveniles commit at least one delinquent act before turning 18, but most are never arrested" (p. 53). Without even attending to those unprocessed cases, the numbers are staggering.

Research supports the notion that youth are starting to commit violent crimes at younger ages (Blumstein, Cohen, & Farrington, 1988). Self-reports of youth who have participated in criminal activities indicate that, at the peak age of 17, approximately 35% have committed at least one serious violent offense (i.e., aggravated assault, robbery, or rape) (Elliott, 1994). Of the juvenile arrests in 1995, about 1 in 7 was for a crime involving violence or the threat of violence (Federal Bureau of Investigation, 1996). In 1994, the rate of violent victimization of juveniles ages 12 to 17 was nearly three times that of adults (Hashima & Finkelhor, 1994). Dryfoos (1990) suggested that, in general, 25% of 10- to 17-year-olds are at high risk for multiple infractions.

Statistics can be both useful and problematic. On one hand, statistics play a significant role in agencies that serve adolescents and families. When applying for federal, state, and local funding through grants, agencies must support claims that services are needed for youth and families. Thus, statistics such as those previously outlined can provide the necessary rationale. A further benefit of statistics is that they stand as a sort of "state of the union" by informing clinicians of national, regional, and local trends regarding the status and severity of juvenile problems.

On the other hand, from a clinical viewpoint, if we were to rely on statistical research alone, we might consider a different line of work. After all, most statistics regarding adolescents point to escalation of crime rates, higher incidences of dropping out of school, increase in drug usage, teenage pregnancy, and overall pathological ways of being. A problem with this view is that numerical representations tell only one side of the story and do not accurately capture the essence of youth. Statistics are statistics—numbers without faces. They do not account for the uniqueness or individuality of adolescents.

When therapists fall under the seductive spell of numbers, they risk developing unhelpful assumptions about youth. As W. O'Hanlon (1990) has discussed with regard to theories, therapists have to beware of "delusions of certainty" or "hardening of the categories" (p. 79)—a belief that they know what the *real* problems are, or, in this case, what the statistics *really* mean. It is important for clinicians to acknowledge the possible benefits of statistics and also to be clear on their limitations. Statistics can open up or close down the possibilities of change.

SURVIVING THE INDUCTION

MOTHER: I don't want him to become another statistic. You know, like another kid gone bad.

THERAPIST: How come he's not already a statistic?

MOTHER: I'm not sure. I guess he's just been lucky.

THERAPIST: Right. It could be luck or something else. It's hard to know for sure. But I wonder what else might be happening with him that has kept him from becoming a number—something that has less to do with luck and more with what he's like as a person.

MOTHER: That's a good question.

This book is about what statistics leave out. Statistics are just one part of any story. Although helpful at times, statistics are based on little doses of information and can lead to unhelpful, broad generalizations and conclusions. As therapists, what we want to do is notice the unnoticed about youth and their situations. This book will help therapists to ask, "What else?"

Interestingly, this question has recently become an important area of research in other fields. For instance, in an attempt to understand how people "miraculously" heal from chronic and terminal illnesses, medical researchers now study that which seems to make a difference for people on a case-by-case basis. This includes taking a second look at cases where unexplained healing and change were previously dismissed as anomalies (Chopra, 1989; Weil, 1995).

What about youth who change and overcome adversity? Let's go back to the case discussed at the very beginning. Although the young man may have been representative of other adolescents and, perhaps, was a statistic in some way, there was more to him than "trouble." Sixteen weeks (nine sessions) after I met this 15-year-old and his mother, the therapy was terminated. Follow-up at one year found that the youth had not had any further involvement with the law. He was continuing to live at home, had obtained a job, and was getting passing grades in all of his classes in school. During a follow-up conversation, the mother talked about her son:

There's a lot more to him than the trouble he had with the law and at home. He's not bad. He had to find his way out of bad behavior and he did. What I'm most happy about is that everybody didn't give up on him. Lots of people did. Even I did. But you guys didn't and he knew you were serious. Now I've got him back. He's got himself back.

This case is not an anomaly. Change of this sort happens every day—inside and outside of therapy. Recently, CBS Television began broadcasting a series entitled *The Class of 2000,* which follows the lives of adolescents who are attempting to deal with very difficult situations. Despite the problems they are facing, these youth are finding ways of transcending them. These adolescents exemplify both the promise of possibility and the importance of resilience.

Michael Rutter (1987) has defined resilience as "the positive role of individual differences in people's responses to stress and adversity" (p. 316). More specifically, resilience relates to situations where a person has lived or grown up in adverse conditions (i.e., low economic resources, underprivileged circumstances, high crime areas, abusive environments) and, despite all that has gone wrong or is still wrong, he or she manages to survive (Herman, 1992; Higgins, 1994; Wolin & Wolin, 1993).

I worked with a young boy, at a local hospital, who had been coming to see various psychiatrists, psychologists, and psychotherapists for over six years. He had been assigned many diagnoses and his problems were deemed "chronic." His mother also had been diagnosed with several psychiatric disorders and was emotionally unstable. His father was a severe alcoholic with an assortment of health problems. There were also familial stressors and financial problems.

This adolescent sought out those people whom he knew he could count on to help: teachers, neighbors, friends, and mental health professionals. He reminded his mother of his appointments. He dealt with her erratic behavior. He helped his father even though he was frequently embarrassed by his episodes of drinking. As if growing up wasn't hard enough, the young man took on whatever challenge faced him and his family.

This youngster became legendary at the hospital for continually being able to deal with adversity. Over and over, he seemed to survive conditions that were unimaginable. He somehow used his own resourcefulness to survive, and in doing so, taught his parents how to do the same.

When we pay attention to what else is present and what makes a difference for adolescents, we can begin to create possibilities for change. Throughout this book, the notion that each adolescent is an exception and has his or her own qualities of resilience will be emphasized. The same holds true for family members and others involved with youth. Milton Erickson (quoted in Zeig, 1980) said, "And so far as I've found in 50 years, every person is a unique individual. I always meet every person as an individual, emphasizing his or her own individual qualities" (p. 220). Youth come from varying circumstances and backgrounds and, ultimately, attention to their uniqueness and to the exceptions in their lives can make a difference. Robert Louis Stevenson said, "Life is not so much a matter of holding good cards, but sometimes of playing a poor hand well." This book is about how to help adolescents and their families play the hand they have and find possibilities when change seems impossible.

This book is also about finding ways of transcending closed-down views and giving adolescents the opportunity to move beyond condemning portrayals such as those highlighted by statistics. I will offer a possibility therapy approach that is collaborative, strength- and resource-focused, respectful, and generally brief.

HOW THIS BOOK IS ARRANGED

Chapter 1, *Traversing the Territory: Foundations of a Possibility Therapy Approach,* begins the journey by taking the reader through four common factors that can facilitate therapy and make a difference for adolescents and families. This is followed by the assumptions of a possibility therapy approach with troubled adolescents, and a discussion about *experience, stories, action,* and *context*—the four different domains that this approach to therapy encompasses.

What Walt Disney Knew: Envisioning the Seemingly Impossible as Possible is next. This chapter discusses the idea of using collaborative language as a way of opening up pathways with possibilities; that is, how we talk about problems, solutions, and possibilities can greatly influence the direction of therapy. Chapter 2 offers ways of conversing with clients that can assist in this process. In addition, ways of getting started by gaining a focus and establishing goals are described.

In Chapter 3, *The Lost Worldview: Evoking New Possibilities in the Realm of Viewing,* the domain of "viewing" is introduced. The chapter explains how therapists can help adolescents and families to shift their views in ways that make possibilities become apparent. The idea of cocreating preferred futures with youth is also described. Through this process, adolescents can envision futures where things work out, then plan out the steps that can make those preferred futures happen.

Chapter 4, *One Thing Leads to Another (Except When It Doesn't): Evoking New Possibilities in the Realms of Action and Context,* moves into the realm of action or the "doing" of problems. It explains how adolescents and families can interrupt unhelpful patterns of action and interaction and create more meaningful and helpful ways of doing things. Ways of working with contextual elements are also offered.

Paving New Roads of Possibility: A Collage of Constructive Conversations, the fifth chapter, offers a number of alternative ways of conversing with adolescents and families. These include finding people who make a difference in adolescents' lives, using self-disclosure, externalizing conversations, the Class of Problems/Class of Solutions model for constructing stories, and the KidsCan approach. Chapter 5 also includes ways of using reflecting teams.

Chapter 6, *The World Where You Live: Rewriting Youth Stories in Future Sessions and Beyond,* begins with discussion of how to approach second and subsequent sessions. Next, ways of maximizing the changes that are attained in and out of therapy are offered. Sharing changes with larger audiences, and having youth track their own progress are two of those ways.

Chapter 7, *Encompassing Angles with Circles: Conversations for Accountability and Change,* delves into the process of promoting accountability among adolescents and their families. This is followed by an exploration of the implications and use of psychiatric labels and psychotropic medications. The chapter concludes with discussions about how to work with adolescents who are mandated to attend therapy, and how to collaborate with larger systems.

As a means of bringing together the ideas presented in the book, Chapter 8, *From End to Beginning: The Case of Richard,* involves the therapy of a 14-year-old adolescent referred for multiple offenses. Edited transcriptions from the entire course of therapy are combined with commentary to illustrate how a possibility therapy approach can be used with adolescents.

The final chapter, *A Return to Yourself: Therapy That Makes a Difference,* discusses how a possibility therapy approach is a way of being with people. Ultimately, this can be helpful in everyday life and in preventing therapist burnout. Chapter 9 also reminds us that just as clients are unique, so are therapists. We have ideas that can be helpful in therapy and ought to let those be heard. The best ideas are often the ones that go unnoticed or unmentioned. Sometimes we have to remember to "reset" ourselves after learning new ideas. We then can bring an array of possibilities to therapy as opposed to only the latest "breakthrough" techniques.

BOB BERTOLINO

St. Charles, Missouri

ACKNOWLEDGMENTS

*T*HANK YOU TO . . .

My family, who have been a constant source of unconditional love and support throughout all my endeavors.

Bill O'Hanlon and Steffanie O'Hanlon, for their help throughout the process of this book, as well as many other projects, and for their friendship, support, and unwavering belief in me.

The following family, friends, and colleagues who made corrections, suggestions, and comments on the manuscript: Christine Bertolino, Pat Holterman-Hommes, John Jaeger, Jennifer Neidner, and Sara Wright.

The staff at Youth in Need, Inc., St. Charles, Missouri, with whom I have had the gift of working since 1989.

My friends, teachers, and colleagues at The Crider Center for Mental Health, Cardinal Glennon Children's Hospital, the Family Development Center, St. Louis University, the University of Missouri-St. Louis, and Lindenwood University.

All the adolescents and families with whom I have worked, for teaching me what I needed to know.

Those whose teachings have greatly influenced me: Bill O'Hanlon, Steve Gilligan, R. Rocco Cottone, Karen Caldwell, John DiTiberio, Nancy Morrison, and Tom Conran.

Milton Erickson and Walt Disney—both of whom I was too young to meet during their lifetimes, but feel connected with in some way.

My musical mates in the bands "11th Hour" and "Drowning Fish," with whom I have played Midwest clubs and recorded music for the past twelve years. Your kinship has been a source of creativity, inspiration, and growth.

Kelly Franklin, Executive Editor and Associate Publisher at John Wiley & Sons, Inc., for taking a chance on me, for always having a nice word to say, and for being a wonderful and insightful person with whom to work.

Dorothy Lin at John Wiley & Sons, Inc., for her assistance with the production of this book.

B. B.

CONTENTS

CHAPTER
ONE

Traversing the Territory

FOUNDATIONS OF A POSSIBILITY
THERAPY APPROACH

*If you have built castles in the air, your work need not
be lost;*

*That is where they should be. Now put the foundations
under them.*

—Henry David Thoreau

A WOMAN CAME TO *therapy with the complaint that she could not "control" her two children. She chose to come alone, at first; she wanted to make sure I was a good choice to be a therapist for her family. After about thirty minutes of conversation, she said, "You must like Elvis Presley." Surprised by her comment (we had not talked about music or anything closely related), I replied, "That's an interesting comment! Yes, I do. But I'm curious about what you're thinking." She went on to say that she had been to four different therapists who had each tried to get her to do things that she had either already tried or that she didn't think were good ideas. For instance, one had sent her to parenting classes, another advised her to get her ex-husband involved, and a third recommended residential placement for her children. She explained that she was not consulted or given a voice as far as what she wanted or thought might work, and was only directed to do various things. The woman told me that what she appreciated about Elvis was that he sang rock and roll, gospel, country, and blues, and was so diverse that all different types and ages of people could appreciate him. She then sat back and said, "I have the feeling that if we listened to rock and roll, that's what you'd use. If we listened to jazz, that's what you'd use. But you wouldn't tell us to listen to opera just because that's what you liked."*

A SHIFT IN FOCUS

Adolescents and their family members are keenly aware of what it's like to be blamed, or seen as having bad intentions, or labeled as resistant. They know what it's like not to be heard or consulted with by so-called "experts," but only told what's wrong in their lives and what to do about it. Truly, adolescents and family members know all too well what it's like to feel hopeless, as if things will never change.

How do these and other invalidating ideas get passed along? The primary way is through the theoretical explanations and verbal constructions that mental health professionals use to define what's

3

wrong with adolescents and families. Many families with adolescents have already heard multiple explanations of what's wrong (i.e., various diagnoses, familial dysfunction, and so on). What they are really seeking is change. In this chapter, I'll discuss how a possibility therapy approach addresses this concern by shifting the focus away from unhelpful and invalidating therapist explanations that close down possibilities, and toward creating change through more collaborative and respectful means. Let's begin our pilgrimage by exploring further why such a shift is necessary and, more specifically, where it leads us.

Explanations, Explanations, Explanations: Who's Buying?

When working with adolescents and their families, it becomes clear that there is no one model of therapy that can fulfill all the needs, circumstances, and complaints that can arise. Thus, it is important that therapists have flexible approaches. But because recent research has shown that most models of psychotherapy produce similar results and there are currently more than 250 models being practiced today, finding an approach that corresponds to a variety of client factors and problems and also offers flexibility can be difficult (Garfield, 1982; Henrink, 1980; Miller, Duncan, & Hubble, 1997).

We must first understand that clients do not buy theories; therapists do. In fact, most adolescents and family members are generally unimpressed with therapists' constructions, yet often find themselves in situations where they are at the mercy of their theoretical explanations. Thus, some parents, in particular, will go along with what therapists have to say, assuming that the therapists know what's best.

With a plethora of psychotherapy theories available, therapists have countless explanations at their fingertips. Virtually all of these explanations and interpretations are valid in some regard. Any problem, whether it involves an individual, a couple, or a family, can have an affective, organic, genetic, psychological, cognitive, interpersonal, social, spiritual, cultural, political, or gender basis—thereby justifying almost any theoretical viewpoint.

On one hand, explanations can provide a normalizing effect for adolescents and families in crisis, and may even lend insight or answers for some. Conversely, theoretical constructions can be invalidating and may convey a sense of hopelessness. When this happens, families can become even more demoralized than they were before they started therapy.

Pros and cons aside, explanations typically do not help families with adolescents to become unstuck. The problem remains even after the therapist has attempted to explain the cause or root of the dysfunction. But if our fascination with explanations does not bode well for adolescents and families in crisis, what do we do? Further, if we don't have a way of explaining things, how do we know where to intervene? Here's a hint: The answer is within.

From Explanation to Change: Milton Erickson

Milton Erickson was a psychiatrist who knew that although clients and patients are less enthusiastic about theories—and in particular, *explanations*—than clinicians are, they are interested in change. Clients want relief. So Erickson shifted attention away from the underpinnings of his previous psychiatric training, which had taught him to explain patients' behavior, to helping them to change it (Gilligan, 1990; Lankton & Lankton, 1983, 1986; W. O'Hanlon, 1987, 1993; W. O'Hanlon & Hexum, 1990).

Erickson demonstrated that *all* approaches have some merit. He would use whatever was helpful in getting his patients unstuck. Among others, Erickson used interventions and methods that were behavioral, psychodynamic, and cognitive (although he was less likely to deem his interventions as theory-specific). He would determine what to use with clients, based on who they were, their personal circumstances, what and how they communicated, and what they wanted to change. Underscoring Erickson's success with a wide range of complaints were his steadfast attention to his patients, and his willingness to learn from them what he needed to know to be of help. This meant treating each patient as a unique individual.

Although Erickson maintained great flexibility with his patients in therapy, he did have *assumptions* that helped to guide his work. He had many ideas about human behavior and theories about how people change—a foundation from which he worked. He was not *theoryless*. But he treated his assumptions as what they were and did not attempt to establish them as *truths*. Erickson worked with his patients to find out what they wanted to change, thereby creating the focus of treatment. He would then evoke and elicit the answers that he believed already existed *within* that person and/or his or her social systems. His work was patient-focused as opposed to theory-focused. The following story illustrates Erickson's emphasis on being patient-focused and evoking answers from within:

When Erickson was a young man, a horse wandered into his yard. Although the horse had no identifying marks, he offered to return it to its owners. To accomplish this, he mounted the horse, led it to the road, and let the horse decide which way it wanted to go. He intervened only when the horse left the road to graze or wander into a field. When the horse finally arrived at the yard of a neighbor several miles down the road, the neighbor asked the young Erickson, "How did you know that horse came from here and was our horse?"

Erickson replied, "I didn't know—but the horse knew. All I did was keep him on the road." (Rosen, 1982, pp. 46–47)

Because he did not subscribe to any one theory, Erickson was not inhibited by theoretical boundaries and guidelines. Today, his work is understood as "strategic," "behavioral," "directive," "indirective," and a host of other things. What, then, was Erickson? The definitive answer to this question depends on with whom you talk. The general answer is that he was all of the descriptions above and many others as well (Combs & Freedman, 1994; Gilligan, 1997a; Haley, 1973; W. O'Hanlon & Weiner-Davis, 1989).

Perhaps the creativity that Erickson demonstrated is the most compelling quality of his work. His focus was on helping his patients to change by use of what were often considered unorthodox means. He did what he felt would help his patients to change, regardless of whether his methods were considered mainstream. I believe this creativity, along with courage, contributed to his success with a wide range of clients and complaints. As Steve Gilligan (1997b) noted, the way Erickson worked can remind us of what is important in the therapeutic milieu:

What was really astonishing about Erickson was his willingness to be himself, to accept his "deviancies" from the norm. This courage translated directly, I believe, into compassion for and acceptance of others. To follow a similar path is remarkably challenging. But this is what we stand for as therapists. (p. 2)

Following in the Footsteps of Erickson and Others

Echoing Gilligan, and following in the spirit of Erickson and in the footsteps of Bill O'Hanlon and others, I will introduce a way of working with adolescents and families that is *change-oriented, respectful, flexible, collaborative,* and *efficient.* Although guided by assumptions, this is not an approach that attempts to explain adolescents' behavior. Rather, it's an orientation that emphasizes the acknowledgment, validation, and valuing of all internal experience while simultaneously helping adolescents and others to move beyond the stuckness they are experiencing in the realms of *views/stories, action,* and *context.* It's also an approach that taps into other therapeutic perspectives in an effort to find what works with clients. Bill O'Hanlon, a former student of Erickson, has dubbed this a *possibility therapy* approach (B. O'Hanlon & Beadle, 1994; S. O'Hanlon & O'Hanlon, 1997; W. O'Hanlon, 1993, 1998).

A possibility therapy approach hinges on the dissolution of theoretical boundaries. To address this, I'd like to offer a musical metaphor.

ESTABLISHING A BASELINE AND FOUNDATION

Toward the Dissolution of Theoretical Boundaries: Four Common Factors

I have played and recorded music since 1985. Over the years, what has become evident to me is that music has become increasingly difficult to categorize. Music in the latter part of the twentieth century is a hybrid of varying textures, rhythms, and melodies. For example, embedded in many forms of rap music are African or Latin rhythms and "classic" rock progressions. In country music, it's also common to hear elements of traditional rock music. Meanwhile, classical music textures can be found in a variety of styles. Because of this blending of various aspects of "traditional" models of music, many new styles have developed (i.e., alternative, hip-hop, ska, and so on). The creativity that is evident in this music reflects ideas from different time periods, cultural backgrounds, and parts of the world.

Perhaps one of the most interesting things about the musical styles today is the complementary way in which varying elements seem to weave together seamlessly to erase previously existing superficial boundaries. The musical elements that are brought together can be identified as distinct and individual entities on their own, and yet they form something that is unique and often refreshingly new. It truly seems that musicians, songwriters, producers, and other members of the musical world have found ways of joining *seemingly* dichotomous elements of musical communities. (Who ever thought they would see Willie Nelson and Beck perform together?)

Unlike musical creators and innovators, some therapists have been slow to acknowledge how ideas from varying theories can work together respectfully. Commonplace within psychotherapy circles has been a tendency to differentiate how theories are dissimilar or "not the same." For a variety of reasons, theorists will stand their ground when it comes to their theoretical constructions. A question is: Who benefits most from efforts to differentiate among theories? One might argue that theorists stand to benefit most because differentiation helps the "selling" of theories. Regardless of what position one chooses, working with adolescents and families requires theoretical flexibility. No one model or theoretical stance will suffice.

Thus, despite "turf" issues in the world of psychotherapy, some theorists have shifted their attention to how theories are similar and may share common threads. In a recent publication, Miller et al. (1997) spoke about how thirty years of psychotherapy research does not support one theory as being more effective than another. Most theories produce similar results. Yet, in cases where positive change does occur with clients and patients, some consistent and common threads can be traced. Miller et al. state:

*The evidence makes it clear that **similarities** rather than **differences** between therapy models account for most of the change that clients experience in treatment. What emerges from examining these similarities is a group of common factors that can be brought together to form* *a more* **unifying language for psychotherapy practice:** *a language that contrasts sharply with the current emphasis on difference characterizing most professional discussion and activity. (p. 15)*

Based on their review of literature, Miller et al. (1997) have outlined four common factors that reflect similarities among theories that seem to make a difference for clients and help them in the process of change (see Table 1.1).

I have expanded these four common factors to reflect a baseline and a foundation for a possibility therapy approach with adolescents and families. These basic foundational assumptions are as follows:

1. *Adolescents and their families have the resources, strengths, and abilities to change—to resolve complaints. The therapist works to elicit, evoke, and highlight these aspects, as opposed to focusing on pathology and deficits.* Part of the therapist's role is to draw out those aspects that can help adolescents to move on. In the evocation of abilities, strengths, and resources, the therapist does not try to convince the youth, or others, of anything. He or she merely highlights those virtues, allowing adolescents to establish their own new meanings, given new or previously unnoticed information. In a possibility therapy approach, the main interventive tool in the elicitation and evocation of adolescents' capacities is language.

2. *The therapist acknowledges, validates, and values adolescents and others involved in the therapeutic process, while promoting accountability.* Adolescents, family members, and others involved need to feel acknowledged and understood. Their feelings, thoughts, and experiences are part of their subjective reality and who they are. Internal experience is all OK, but not all actions are OK (i.e., stealing, hurting others, and so on). This means that youth can feel what they feel, experience what they experience, and remain accountable for their actions and behaviors (Bertolino, 1998a; B. O'Hanlon, 1996a; B. O'Hanlon & Bertolino, 1998).

3. *Consideration is given to how aspects or ideas of differing theoretical perspectives can be unified to benefit adolescents and families.* A current debate in the field of psychotherapy is whether therapists should use "pure" models or move toward those that are more integrative. There are strengths and weaknesses on both sides

TABLE 1.1
FOUR COMMON FACTORS

1. *The total matrix of clients.* Miller et al. (1995, 1997) have estimated that, in cases where there is improvement, approximately 40% of the change can be related to client factors. They refer to these as "extratherapeutic factors"—the person's strengths, resources, social supports, and environments, and the type (frequency, intensity, and duration) of the complaints the person has.

2. *The therapeutic relationship.* The effects of the client–therapist relationship can contribute as much as 30% to outcome (Lambert, 1992). Clients who are engaged and connected with the therapist may benefit the most from therapy. Additionally, a therapist who is empathic, genuine, and respectful contributes to a positive bind or alliance with the therapist (Rogers, 1951, 1961). Perhaps most important are clients' perceptions of the therapist as being warm, empathic, trustworthy, and nonjudgmental (Miller et al., 1995, 1997).

3. *Therapeutic technique.* Most models of therapy make use of procedures or techniques that are employed to help clients take some action to help themselves. These can include: developing new understandings or meanings, experiencing emotions, facing fears, altering patterns of behavior, and so on. The content of the discussion or questions may differ, depending on the clinician's perspective, orientation, or technique. Nevertheless, inherent to each theory is a way of helping clients via specific processes (Miller et al., 1995, 1997). Lambert (1992) estimates that therapeutic models and techniques contribute 15% in cases where client change occurs.

4. *Expectancy, hope, and placebo.* In relation to outcome, placebo factors can make the same percentagewise contribution (about 15%) as techniques in the change process (Miller et al., 1995, 1997). The placebo effect refers to an increased expectation for change that clients experience simply from beginning treatment. The therapist's attitude in the opening moments of therapy greatly influences clients' expectations for change. Therapists' attitudes emphasizing possibilities and the belief that things can work can help build hope for clients. Conversely, attitudes of pessimism, an emphasis on psychopathology, or the long-term nature of change can adversely affect clients.

Adapted and modified from *Escape from Babel: Toward a Unifying Language for Psychotherapy Practice,* by Scott Miller, Barry Duncan, and Mark Hubble, New York: Norton, 1997.

of this debate, and the voices of clients often remain unheard. This is a debate among theorists, not clients. In a possibility therapy approach, emphasis is on finding ideas that complement one another to provide the best possible fit, given the uniqueness of each case. Therapists find what works and avoid "negatively hallucinating" or casting aside ideas that their theories are "allergic" to. Thus, a possibility therapy approach is more of an *inclusive* rather than an integrative approach. That is, the parts work together to benefit adolescents and families but are distinguished from one another and are not considered exclusive to any one approach.

4. *Therapists maintain a belief in and a focus on change.* A common myth that is often retold to adolescents today is that they do not have the ability to change or are incapable of changing. Acceptance of the myth is invalidating to youth and unhelpful for therapists. It is incumbent that therapists believe that change is possible. Milton Erickson often said to his patients, "I don't know how you're going to change." He insinuated that they *would* change. He merely left it open for each person to determine how the change would come about.

This baseline, comprised of common factors, can promote the change process and incorporate what seems to make a difference for clients in therapy. These common factors also represent a respectful way of working with troubled teenagers and their families. With the baseline as a starting point, we can begin to move toward theoretical contributions and further assumptions of a possibility therapy approach.

POSSIBILITY THERAPY ASSUMPTIONS

In December 1996, I went to Santa Fe, New Mexico, to visit Bill and Steffanie O'Hanlon. During the visit, we took a walk on a nearby road that overlooks the mountains and offers a breathtaking view. We talked about how therapists sometimes become so enamored of their theories that they become hypnotized by them. When this happens, they can see only their theories; other ideas are negatively hallucinated (something that is physically present is not seen), even though they may have been previously helpful. What is positively hallucinated (something that isn't physically present is seen) is a single, restrictive way of viewing or thinking about things—the *way to do therapy*. For clients, and particularly those raising adolescents, this restrictive view can be very unhelpful; they do not get the full benefit of what the therapist may have to offer (i.e., personal or professional experience, training, and so on). Instead, families get the "latest breakthrough" in therapeutic technique or the newest theory with which the therapist has fallen in love.

Many therapists have ideas, interventions, and techniques that work very well in their practice. It is important to hold on to these ideas! The assumptions of a possibility therapy approach build on therapists' already existing knowledge and experience. Thus, this approach is meant to complement, not replace, what clinicians are already doing.

The following ten underlying assumptions, along with the four baseline factors outlined previously, are meant to keep therapy respectful, collaborative, flexible, and, I believe, generally briefer with adolescents and families. These assumptions will be expanded on during the course of the book.

1. *Therapy is a collaborative endeavor*. Duncan, Hubble, and Miller (1997a) stated, "Impossibility, we decided, is at least partly a function of leaving clients out of the process, of not listening or of dismissing the importance of their perspective" (p. 30). Therapy with adolescents and families is a collaborative venture. Throughout the entire process of therapy, adolescents and family members are consulted about goals, directions, and the methods being used. Ideas and questions are "offered" to adolescents and families in a nonauthoritarian way. They have the space to agree or disagree with, modify, or correct what has been said or done. In addition, a collaborative stance is extended to outside helpers (i.e., juvenile officers, teachers, friends, and so on) who may be involved in the therapy. If discouraging ideas originate from outside helpers, the therapist will gently and subtly challenge those unhelpful ideas by first acknowledging their possible validity and then introducing alternative perspectives (S. O'Hanlon & O'Hanlon, 1997). The therapist's first loyalty remains with the adolescent and family.

2. *Multiple realities, stories, and truths are respected*. Parry and Doan (1994) relate that there is no one claim to truth that is

respected above all others, and "no single story sums up the meaning of life" (p. 10). There is no one *correct* way to view the world because there are as many realities as there are people on earth. Craig Smith (1997) remarked:

> No one can form a complete, panoramic, exhaustive view of reality or of the problems clients bring to therapy. Each person involved in the problem scenario would be seen as having a valid yet partial perceptual claim or explanation for what the problem is and what should be done about it. (p. 29)

In regard to youth, Erickson (1958/1980) stated, "young people . . . define the world and its events in a different way than does the adult" (p. 174). And while it is important to be sensitive to the different ways that adolescents view the world, it is also important to discern those that may be harmful or dangerous to self and/or others. In instances where there is such risk, the therapist must take appropriate action to avoid harmful consequences (Bertolino, 1998a).

3. *The therapist and each member of the client system are cocreators of the reality within the therapeutic context.* There is a physical reality, but subjective reality is observer-defined. Bateson (1972) related that the belief system a person has "about what sort of world it is will determine how he sees it and acts within it, and his ways of perceiving and acting will determine his beliefs about its nature" (p. 314). Clients' worldviews are primarily influenced by biology and personal experiences (i.e., social interactions). The same holds true for therapists, who must also contend with theoretical maps and constructions that can greatly alter the course of treatment (Efran & Lukens, 1985).

Therapy takes place in the domain of language and social interaction (Berger & Luckmann, 1966). Interpersonal relationships and interactions with others contribute to identities' being formed and reformed. We live in different realities, with different people, at different times, yet reality is cocreated between the therapist and each member of the client system within the therapeutic milieu.

A therapist who maintains the view that change is possible can convey this belief through the use of language and interaction. This, in turn, can contribute to the cocreation of new, less oppressive narratives. Conversely, therapists who are guided by pathology or unhelpful assumptions that close down possibilities for change can create or reinforce narratives in which little or nothing seems possible.

4. *The construction of meaning and the taking of action are essential considerations.* A wave of new therapies considers the generation of new meaning on the part of the client to be a primary goal of therapy (Andersen, 1991; Anderson & Goolishian, 1988). It is suggested that when clients develop new meanings, their problems will be resolved. This is a shift from interactional approaches that focus mainly on action and interaction.

There are two considerations here. First, not all families will change by simply gaining new meaning in their lives. Saleeby (1994) commented that after people have established some new meaning, they should be encouraged to "begin to create a vision about what might be and to take some steps to achieve it" (p. 357). This is especially important to consider with adolescents. Often, youth and family members will need to take action to obtain the change they desire.

A second consideration is that when meaning leads to new action, the process can be reciprocal; that is, new action may lead to the generation of new meaning. Thus, to focus solely on the domain of meaning or the domain of action necessitates leaving out something that may ultimately assist in the resolution of a complaint. A possibility therapy approach stands in accordance with Thomas Eron and Joseph Lund (1996), who commented, "Effective therapeutic conversations enter the realms of story *and* frame; address meaning and action; and, by so doing, help to resolve problems" (p. 38).

5. *The therapist and the members of the therapeutic system have expertise.* The therapist stakes no claim to preconstructed knowledge resulting from methods and/or theory (Bobele, Gardner, & Biever, 1995) and is not considered an expert on interpreting others' experiences. Therapists have ideas that are based on education and experience; however, adolescents and family members have unique expertise. They know what is going on in their lives, what their concerns are, what hasn't worked, and what feels respectful or disrespectful. It is both respectful and collaborative to allow the expertise of clients to emerge in therapy. By allowing each person's

story to evolve, the therapist can be taught by adolescents, and others, what he or she needs to know.

The therapist's expertise is in creating a context that is conducive to the change process. This includes establishing a safe atmosphere where adolescents' and family members' stories can evolve, and helping, through conversation and/or action, to access new pathways that offer possibilities. Metaphor, stories, ideas, and thoughts are *offered,* not imposed, as part of an ongoing therapist and youth/family dialogue.

6. *Emphasis is on making the most of each session.* Research has demonstrated that, regardless of the theoretical model employed, the modal number of sessions that clients attend is one (Hoyt, 1994b; Rosenbaum, Hoyt, & Talmon, 1990; Talmon, 1990). Often, people get what they came for in just one meeting. If this sounds strange, one need only look at general practitioners in the medical profession. When a person visits a doctor, he or she is treated for the presenting complaint. A return or follow-up visit is scheduled only if needed. Therapists can learn from medical doctors that attention ought to focus on what the patient or client is complaining about. In psychotherapy, efficient work toward searching for openings with possibilities for solution and change is the respectful, practical, and ethical position.

7. *Orientation is toward the present and future.* Erickson (1954) remarked, "Emphasis should be placed more upon what the patient does in the present and will do in the future than upon a mere understanding of why some long-past event occurred" (p. 127). When adolescents feel understood in the here and now, doors with possibilities for the future can become more apparent. This does not dismiss the possible significance of past events. If youth or others are oriented toward the past, the therapist should be respectful and follow them where they need to go. However, the clinician does not hold the assumption that this is how adolescents need to resolve their conflicts. It is believed that most youth and families, when given the choice, will opt to see their problems dissipate in the present rather than review humiliating or unsatisfying events of the past. Thus, there is no preconceived theory mandating that underlying pathologies must be resolved before an adolescent can move on.

8. *Adolescents and their families define desired change and goals.* Youth and their families determine what needs to be different in their lives—where they want to go. They are experts on their lives; they generally know what is best for themselves. But there are exceptions. An obvious one is the establishment of illegal goals such as child abuse, discrimination, or committing crimes; another is the setting of unrealistic or unachievable goals. In the latter case, the therapist must work within the therapeutic system to establish more feasible and attainable goals. When realistic goals are established through a collaborative process, therapists know where to intervene and help clients to create possibilities.

9. *It is not necessary to know a great deal about a complaint, or the cause or function of it, to resolve it.* People solve problems every day. Some go to therapy, some don't. Ironically, problem resolution rarely has anything to do with the explanations that people give for the causes and reasons for their problems. If it did, they wouldn't need to attend therapy—they could explain their problems away. A concern for therapists is that families with adolescents may desire to know the cause of their son's or daughter's problem; often, a cause is not easy to pinpoint. Interestingly, most families will gladly abandon their search for explanations once their complaint has been resolved.

As therapists, we know that change is constant, and we are aware that problem resolution without the use of explanations can be rapid *and* lasting. It's not possible for us to *discover what the "real" problems* are with people. That's too subjective and biased, given that we can consult only our own realities and theoretical constructions. What we can do is work with adolescents and others to determine what has or hasn't worked for them, and explore avenues of change that do not involve explaining behaviors.

10. *Therapy takes as long as it does.* A common argument in psychotherapy circles is whether therapy should be brief or long-term. Research indicates that the average length of clients' attendance in therapy is six to ten sessions (Doherty & Simmons, 1996; Garfield, 1989; Koss & Butcher, 1986; Levitt, 1966; Miller, 1994). Miller et al. (1997) wrote that "all large-scale meta-analytic studies of client change indicate that the most frequent improvement occurs early in

treatment" (p. 194). Studies have shown that most major positive impact in therapy happens during the first six to eight sessions, and continuing but decreasing impact occurs over the next ten sessions (M. Smith, Glass, & Miller, 1980; Talmon, 1990).

Managed care and funding restrictions necessitate that therapists become more efficient, but research shows that clients attend only a handful of sessions regardless of a therapist's orientation. Following the example of general medical practitioners, therapists must work to maximize the effectiveness of each session in helping adolescents and their families to resolve their concerns as quickly as possible. Granted, some clients will need one, two, or five sessions, and others will need thirty sessions. From a possibility therapy perspective, it is not the number of sessions that is most important, but collaborating with adolescents and families to determine where they want to go, when things are better, and when goals have been met. This approach, by nature, makes therapy generally briefer and consumer-based.

These ten assumptions serve as a *guide* for therapists working with adolescents and families. It is my belief that these ideas facilitate and enhance the change process. Rather than working to explain what is happening with people, therapists can learn from clients what they would like to be different in their lives, creating a place to intervene. Then, therapists can work to evoke and elicit strengths, abilities, and resources, while changing clients' views/stories and actions, and the contexts in which their problems linger. These domains are discussed next.

EXPERIENCE, VIEWS/STORIES, ACTIONS, AND CONTEXT

From a possibility therapy perspective, therapy with adolescents and families is seen as involving four different domains: *(a) experience, (b) views/stories, (c) action,* and *(d) context.* Table 1.2 offers an outline of these domains.

Experience relates to that which happens internally—a person's feelings, sensations, fantasies, and anything else that contributes to

TABLE 1.2 REALMS OF INTERVENTION			
Experience	**Views/Stories**	**Actions**	**Context**
Feelings	Points of view	Action patterns	Time patterns
Sense of self	Attentional patterns	Interactional patterns	Spatial patterns
Bodily sensations	Interpretations	Language patterns	Cultural background and propensities
Sensory experience	Explanations	Nonverbal patterns	
	Evaluations		Family/ Historical background and propensities
Automatic fantasies and thoughts	Assumptions		
	Beliefs		Biochemical/ Genetic background and propensities
	Identity stories		
			Gender training and propensities

Copyright © 1996 by Bill O'Hanlon.

the person's sense of self. Experience is very subjective and personalized. Throughout this book, it will be emphasized that all internal experience is OK.

Views come in two varieties. The first relates to what people orient their attention toward or in their own lives or situations, or in reference to other's lives or situations. The views that people hold can become troublesome when attention is paid, largely or solely, to problematic aspects of their lives while other more helpful or less oppressive aspects go unnoticed.

The second type of view is *stories* (e.g., beliefs, assumptions, explanations) which are based on people's perceptions, understandings, and constructions of meaning. *Stories* or narratives are how people describe themselves and others. Stories are changeable and subject to continual renegotiation. Stories do not symbolize truth;

they represent a person's perception of the world, created through experience and interaction. Some stories are supportive and spawn hope. Others are problematic or problem-saturated; in them, the possibility of change seems almost nonexistent.

Actions are what the person actually does. As mentioned earlier, some actions are OK and others are not. Actions that help clients to achieve their goals and are healthy, legal, and ethical are OK. Actions or behaviors that move clients away from their goals and are unhealthy or harmful, illegal, or unethical are not acceptable.

Context involves aspects of a person's history and background, including cultural, genetic, biochemical, familial, gender, and spatial and timing patterns. These contextual aspects can be problematic in their creation or support of a problem, or supportive, with helpful aspects sometimes being buried and unnoticed.

Throughout this book, numerous ways of acknowledging the internal experiences of youth while creating possibilities in the domains of stories, action, and context will be discussed. In the next chapter, ways that therapists can work with adolescents and families in creating a collaborative context are offered. I also discuss how to begin therapy from a possibility therapy perspective.

CHAPTER TWO

What Walt Disney Knew

ENVISIONING THE SEEMINGLY IMPOSSIBLE AS POSSIBLE

You see things, and you say "Why?"; but I dream things that never were, and I say "Why not?"

—Bernard Shaw

Always listen to experts. They'll tell you what can't be done and why. Then do it.

—Robert Heinlein

*O*N DECEMBER 15, 1966, *at the age of 65, Walt Disney passed away. That evening, in a moving tribute, CBS news correspondent Eric Sevareid said, "He probably did more to heal or at least to soothe troubled human spirits than all the psychiatrists in the world. . . . What Walt Disney seemed to know was that while there is very little grown-up in a child, there is a lot of child in every grown-up." (Thomas, 1994, p. 355)*

One of the most compelling things about Walt Disney was the way that he envisioned life. Whether making cartoons or feature films, developing new artistic or musical media, or building theme parks, he was in a constant state of exploring what was possible. Disney figured that if you can dream something, you can make it a reality.

For example, when Disneyland was being constructed in California, Walt would often take park engineers to the site to discuss his ideas with them. During these meetings, it was common for him to convey what he had planned for a certain attraction or aspect of the park, which was sometimes outlandish, and for one or more of the engineers to say, "Walt, we can't do that. It won't work." But Walt was persistent. He had a clear vision of how he thought Disneyland ought to be. So he would ask his engineers to kneel down, view a certain aspect of the park, and tell him what they saw. Why? Because he felt it was the best way to get the engineers to experience the perspective of the children who would be coming to the park. Once the engineers understood the importance of the vision, they would figure out how to make what was seemingly impossible possible. Time after time, Disney and his engineers would turn visions into reality.

What can we learn from this? Two things. First, although we are not creating theme parks here, when we hold the belief that change can happen with adolescents in *even the most difficult situations,* the seemingly impossible can become possible. Just as Disney focused on what was possible, therapists can orient toward the possibilities of change.

As previously noted, therapists' attitudes, particularly in the opening moments of therapy, can greatly influence clients' expectation for change (Miller et al., 1997). Therapists who emphasize possibilities and a belief that things can work can help build hope for clients. Conversely, pessimism, or an emphasis on psychopathology or on the long-term nature of change, can adversely affect clients. This is crucial because, in many instances, youth and their families have already directly or indirectly been sent the message that their situations are "impossible." An attitude that people cannot change is not only invalidating, it's counterproductive.

This approach does not in any way downplay the problems that adolescents and their families experience. This is not about being a Pollyanna. I am not suggesting that if we have our clients "wish upon a star," say enough affirmations, or think "positive," everything will be just fine and all their problems will evaporate into thin air. Troubled adolescents and their families experience very difficult and debilitating problems. I am suggesting that we can acknowledge and attend to their circumstances, difficulties, and problems without closing down the possibilities for change.

A second thing we can learn from Walt Disney is the idea of *collaboration*. Although he had some strong opinions about Disneyland, Walt learned to read architectural drawings so he could understand what the engineers were talking about when they referred to designs. He could then communicate with them in a common language. Sometimes one or the other would have to slightly shift an earlier vision, but Walt and his engineers were always able to negotiate an achievable reality and end. Disney also worked collaboratively with numerous others in developing new methods of filming, improved audio soundtrack recording, animatronics, and many more significant innovations. A possibility therapy perspective views collaboration as a crucial starting and ongoing part of the therapy process. How and to what degree adolescents and their families are involved can greatly influence the direction of therapy. Further, how others, such as relatives, teachers, and juvenile officers, are involved can make a difference.

As discussed in Chapter 1, collaboration takes on many forms in a possibility therapy approach. Perhaps most important is its role in the medium that therapists most rely on—conversation. The significance of conversation in possibility therapy cannot be understated.

The ways clinicians talk with adolescents and others about their problems and situations can greatly influence their perceptions and, ultimately, the change process. Client–therapist dialogues can either inhibit or promote change. From a possibility therapy perspective, collaborative conversations are designed to promote change. The following section describes ways of dialoguing collaboratively with youth and families and outlines the contrasts with traditional types of conversation.

COLLABORATIVE CONVERSATIONS: A MEDIUM FOR CHANGE

Traditional Conversations

Many traditional approaches to therapy with adolescents rely on conversations that are designed to explain or interpret verbal and nonverbal communication to promote insight or understanding, invite the expression of emotion, or uncover mental illness and pathological processes. Therapists are held as experts, and clients are considered nonexperts and put into a one-down position. These kinds of ideas tend to close down avenues of change and can be disrespectful of adolescents and their families (see Table 2.1).

Collaborative Conversations

A possibility therapy approach moves away from traditional types of conversations to dialogues that value people in the therapeutic process. Therapists, youth, and family members are all considered experts. Adolescents and family members have expertise in their own experiences, and therapists, through conversation and interaction, are experts in creating a climate that is conducive to change. Therapists, along with adolescents and their families, are partners in the therapeutic process.

To create a climate that values clients and promotes change, therapists rely on the use of collaborative conversations. Bill O'Hanlon (1993) has discussed the idea of collaborative conversations and has described six different forms, as outlined in Table 2.2. These types of conversations underlie a possibility therapy approach from beginning to end.

TABLE 2.1
TRADITIONAL CONVERSATIONS

❖ *Conversations for explanations.*

Searching for evidence of functions for problems.

Searching for or encouraging searches for causes, and giving or supporting messages about determinism (biological/ developmental/psychological).

Focusing or allowing a focus on history as the most relevant part of the adolescent's life.

Engaging in conversations for determining diagnosis, categorization, and characterization.

Supporting or encouraging conversations for identifying pathology.

❖ *Conversations for inability.*

❖ *Conversations for insight/understanding.*

❖ *Conversations for expressions of emotion.*

Eliciting adolescent's expressions of feelings, and focusing on feelings.

❖ *Conversations for blame and recrimination.*

Attributions of bad/evil personality or bad/evil intentions.

❖ *Adversarial conversations.*

The therapist believes that adolescents have hidden agendas that keep them from cooperating with treatment goals/methods.

Using trickery/deceit to get the client to change.

The therapist is the expert and clients are nonexperts.

Adapted and modified from the work of Bill O'Hanlon. Copyright © 1996e by Bill O'Hanlon.

TABLE 2.2
COLLABORATIVE CONVERSATIONS

❖ *Conversations for change/difference.*

Highlighting changes that have occurred in adolescents' problem situations.

Presuming change will happen/is happening.

Searching for descriptions of differences in the problem situation.

Introducing new distinctions or highlighting distinctions with adolescents.

❖ *Conversations for competence/abilities.*

Presuming adolescent competence/ability.

Searching for contexts of competence away from the problem situation.

Eliciting descriptions of exceptions to the problem, or times when adolescents dealt with the problem situation in a way they liked.

❖ *Conversations for possibilities.*

Focusing the conversation on the possibilities of the future/goals/visions.

Introducing new possibilities for doing/viewing into the problem situation.

❖ *Conversations for goals/results.*

Focusing on how adolescents/families/court authorities, and so on, will know that they've achieved their therapeutic goals.

❖ *Conversations for accountability/personal agency.*

Holding adolescents/others accountable for their actions.

Presuming actions derive from adolescents' intentions/selves.

❖ *Conversations for action descriptions.*

Channeling the conversation about the problem situation into action descriptions.

Changing characterizational/theoretical talk into descriptive words.

Focusing on actions adolescents/others can take that make a difference in the problem situation.

Adapted and modified from the work of Bill O'Hanlon. Copyright © 1996e by Bill O'Hanlon.

Collaborative forms of dialoguing with adolescents, family members, and others allow therapists to remain in the competency domain and orient toward possibilities and change as opposed to pathology and deficits. They also help to keep therapy client-driven, respectful, and goal-focused while simultaneously inviting accountability.

We've now talked about the role of common factors among theories of psychotherapy that establish a baseline. We've also talked about assumptions associated with a possibility therapy approach, the importance of having a change orientation, and being collaborative through conversation. With all of these things considered, we can begin to address the question: How does therapy begin? In discussing this question, we must consider two others: (a) Whom should the therapist see in therapy? (b) What about assessment?

WHOM TO SEE?

We know that change in one part of a system effects change in other parts of that system. Erickson believed that small changes could produce a snowball-like effect and lead to bigger changes. In fact, he would often work with just one person from a family or one member of a couple and obtain profound changes. Yet, many traditional forms of family therapy maintain that it is necessary to work with an entire family when adolescents in that family are experiencing trouble.

It is not necessary to see an entire family for a situation to change. From a possibility therapy approach, whoever comes to therapy is the person(s) with whom the therapist ought to work. At the initial session, I *prefer* to see the parent or guardian and the adolescent. In this way, I can make sure that each person feels acknowledged and understood and that all concerns are heard. Occasionally, a parent will show up for the first appointment without his or her son or daughter. At other times, an adolescent will be brought in for the initial session by a parent, grandparent, or other person, who then leaves. I proceed by seeing whoever comes in. However, when a parent or other person drops off a youth, I always contact the parent and schedule a time to meet, so that I can be clear about all parties' expectations of therapy.

After the first meeting, I see families in various combinations. Therapy can consist of sessions with intact families, parts of families, or just one person. It can include relatives, teachers, juvenile officers, friends, and anyone who may be helpful in the situation (with the family's consent, of course). Therapy sessions can also be split up, with each person being seen individually, in dyads, in triads, and so on. For example, at times I will meet with a mother for twenty minutes and then with her son or daughter for thirty minutes. Or, I will meet with both together for fifteen minutes and then meet with just one of them for the remainder of the session. Although my experience has been that most families generally do not have a preference about how they want to meet, some parents expect that their son or daughter will be seen alone. It is both respectful and collaborative to consult with family members during the first meeting, to see what their expectations may be.

Some practitioners worry about deviance from the "traditional" idea of seeing families as whole units. I'm not concerned about coalitions or having covert alliances. There are alliances and they are all overt. The goal is to connect with each family member in some way. Each person must feel heard and understood, and that is not always possible in large families without using varying meeting arrangements.

For those in search of more specific ways of deciding whom to include in therapy, the following questions may be helpful: Who is complaining? Who thinks there is a problem? Who is willing to pay for therapy and/or do something to effect change? What concerns will constrain or affect therapy? Who is pushing for change? (S. O'Hanlon & O'Hanlon, 1997).

Everyone's a Customer

Some therapists have advocated a method of assessing customership among clients. This translates to labeling clients as being *customers* because they are "willing" and want to do something to resolve a complaint, or *visitors* because they have come to therapy without a complaint or unwillingly (de Shazer, 1988). Selekman (1997) has remarked that most adolescents are visitors, because someone other than themselves is requesting that they change. Still others are deemed *complainants* because they are concerned or worried about someone else's behaviors (de Shazer, 1985).

In regard to this solution-focused therapy (SFT) method of compartmentalizing clients, Jefferson Fish (1997) recently commented that SFT practitioners might have been basing their high rate of success on only those cases where there was a customer. Fish remarked that, if this is the case:

> A central issue becomes how well [SFT] does at converting complainants—who lack that motivation—to customers. As an empirical issue, this is open to investigation. As a clinical issue, the question becomes what to do with complainants who remain complainants after reasonable solution-focused efforts. One solution-focused response is to terminate and wish them well. (p. 269)

A possibility therapy approach does not face this dilemma because it does not rest on the customer/visitor/complainant schematic. Although many adolescents do not want to be in therapy and let the therapist know this in one way or another, they are motivated for something (not having to come to therapy!) and are customers. Duncan, Hubble, and Miller (1997b) stated:

> There is no such individual as an unmotivated client. Clients may not, as we have found all too often, share ours, but they certainly hold strong motivations of their own. An unproductive and futile therapy can come about by mistaking or overlooking what the client wants to accomplish, misapprehending the client's readiness for change, or pursuing a personal motivation. (p. 11)

Most assuredly, some participants in therapy will be more helpful, and perhaps, more invested in the change process than others. However, from a possibility therapy perspective, everyone is considered a customer. The therapist's task is to determine what each customer hopes to have happen or change.

What about Assessment?

It is commonplace for mental health settings that serve adolescents and families to use a universal or specific assessment to gather information. Some places will require only minimal information: demographic data and a brief social history. Others will require completion of in-depth, lengthy, and rather complex assessment tools, often as a prelude to psychiatric diagnosis for an adolescent. Given the variety of circumstances that can arise, there are two considerations that I will address:

1. *From a possibility therapy perspective, assessment is not a one-time affair.* It is ongoing. Assessment begins when therapy starts, and it continues throughout, as established goals are met, modified, and changed. Adolescents and families, and their problems, are not static.

2. *Assessment does not translate to simply discovering or uncovering pathology.* In recent years, with an emphasis on more collaborative and competency-based approaches, clinicians have created innovative ways of interviewing clients for not just problems, deficits, and limitations, but also for strengths, abilities, and resources (Berg, 1994; Durrant, 1993, 1995; B. O'Hanlon, 1996b; Selekman, 1997).

Should a particular setting require that a certain type of pathology-based assessment be completed, a respectful and collaborative approach is to let the adolescent and family members know that every client goes through the same or a similar procedure. This information normalizes the process; the therapist can complete the required assessment and then move to a more competency-based focus. Here are a couple of examples of how to introduce adolescents and families to assessment procedures:

There are some questions that I need to ask you—that we ask of everyone who comes here. I'll begin with some questions that will tell me about what's going on that's a problem for you. Once we get through those questions, we'll move on to some others that will tell me more about what you do well and what works.

There are two parts to this interview. The first part will involve questions that will give us an idea of how things have become troublesome. The second part will allow us to talk in a different way about your situation.

Some assessments may be pathology- or problem-focused, but they allow room for the therapist to ask other questions that introduce some sort of balance, and they work to elicit and evoke competencies and resources. For example, a therapist can ask about the problem and then inquire about exceptions or past successes. In this approach, information can be garnered simultaneously about strengths, abilities, and resources as well as problem areas. This sample dialogue shows how a therapist might go about this:

THERAPIST: What school do you go to?

ADOLESCENT: Gardner High.

THERAPIST: What grade are you in?

ADOLESCENT: Tenth.

THERAPIST: What's school like for you?

ADOLESCENT: It's OK now.

PARENT: But she was suspended for 34 days last year for fighting.

THERAPIST: Were those days all in a row or separate suspensions?

ADOLESCENT: I was suspended seven times. Once for ten days and all the others were for four days each.

THERAPIST: How come you didn't get thrown out of school for so many fights?

ADOLESCENT: Most of them were at the beginning of the year, and I only had one after Christmas.

THERAPIST: Really? How did you manage to change things around?

ADOLESCENT: I like school. It was just this one girl that I fought. She's cool now.

Even when the information seems to be very problematic, the therapist can consider, "What else?" These are sometimes referred to as *exception* questions (de Shazer, 1988, 1991; W. O'Hanlon & Weiner-Davis, 1989; Selekman, 1993). They ask for information about when a problem is less dominating, occurs less frequently, is absent, and so on. In turn, the information gathered can form building blocks for client change. Here are some examples of questions that search for exceptions:

❖ It seems that when this problem is happening, things are pretty difficult. When does the problem seem less noticeable to you? What is everyone doing when it's less noticeable?

❖ When does the problem appear to happen less?

❖ What do you suppose keeps your son/daughter from going off the deep end with trouble?

❖ What is your son/daughter doing when he/she is not in trouble?

❖ Tell me what it's like when the problem is a little less dominating.

❖ What's it like when things are a bit more manageable?

Notice that these questions do not inquire about extremes. They don't ask: "When don't you have the problem?" That's too big a leap for most adolescents and family members. Instead, these questions work to elicit small exceptions. All we are searching for is a thread of hope or a ray of light. That can be enough to get the ball rolling.

By asking exception-oriented questions along with the ones that are required on the mandated assessment tool, the interviewer can gain valuable information from the adolescent and family. In addition, hope can be injected into what can often be a very negative experience for youth. If therapy involves focusing only on everything that is or has gone wrong with an adolescent, it can be further invalidating and will replicate what the client has already heard on countless occasions. The same caution can hold true for parents; they may feel that they have failed, given what they have had to reveal or describe in the assessment.

Other than asking a few demographic and informational questions, clinicians can usually gather the necessary information by following the process outlined later in the chapter. The youth and others can be heard through their personal accounts.

For those who are in need of more specific exception-oriented information, here are some possible assessment questions:

The Problem

- ❖ When do you seem to get more of an upper hand with your problem and be not so pushed around by your behavior? How do you do that?

- ❖ When things are going poorly, how does your son/daughter usually start/stop his/her unacceptable behavior? To help the situation, what do you do that's different?

- ❖ What have others failed to notice about your situation or problem?

School

- ❖ What's something that you can tolerate about school and maybe even enjoy about it sometimes?

- ❖ Which of your teachers do you get along with best? (Or: Which of your teachers drives you the least crazy?)

- ❖ How have you managed to pass in previous years? (Or: . . . pass *any* class . . . if the youth failed all but one, for instance.)

Police and Court History

- ❖ How come you're not already locked up?

- ❖ How have you managed to keep from getting into further trouble with the police?

- ❖ What's the longest you've gone without being in trouble with the law? How did you do that?

Social Relationships

- ❖ Who recognizes that you have something else to offer, other than the problem for which you're here?

- ❖ Whom can you go to when you need help?

- ❖ When are your friends most helpful to you?

- ❖ What people have you met who have made a positive difference in your life?

Previous Therapy Experiences

❖ What has been helpful about previous experiences in therapy?

❖ What made a difference for you?

❖ What wasn't so helpful?

General Questions

❖ What is it that other people don't know about you?

❖ What do you want other people to know about you?

Therapists can cover many areas with exception-based questions during an initial assessment. Because a possibility orientation views assessment as an ongoing process, these questions can be helpful at any point during therapy.

Avoiding Theory Countertransference

Inherent to assessment procedures and therapeutic methods are ideas that can close down pathways of possibilities. Traditions are important in all human pursuits, but they can also inhibit change or even have damaging consequences (Duncan et al., 1997b). Hubble and O'Hanlon (1992) have deemed clinicians' loyalties to theoretical constructs as "theory countertransference." They state:

> Unfortunately, most therapists have what we call "delusions of certainty" or "hardening of the categories." They are convinced that the observations they make during the assessment process are "real" and objective. They are certain they have discovered *real* problems. . . . Lacking from the discussion of countertransference in the psychoanalytic literature has been much examination of the ways in which the therapist's "theory" influences the work. While it was widely accepted that the person of the psychoanalyst . . . could be facilitative or disruptive, less attention was paid to how the clinician's overall conception of the human condition and therapy would affect treatment outcomes. (pp. 25–27)

Assessment, often considered *the* starting point of therapy, is, from this perspective, ongoing. The therapist must beware of how his or her theoretical constructs influence the content, process, and direction of therapy. Truly, the therapist will have ideas, thoughts, and theories. The same is true for adolescents, parents, other family members, outside helpers, and so on. Clients' points of view must be acknowledged from the start of therapy and throughout the process, or the situation can close down quickly. The premise here is that, by remaining in a collaborative relationship, all ideas can be considered without any one viewpoint or reality taking precedence over the others.

TELL ME A STORY: BEGINNING THERAPY

As with solution-oriented and solution-focused approaches, in a possibility approach, therapy begins when someone complains about something (de Shazer, 1988, 1991; O'Hanlon & Weiner-Davis, 1989; Walter & Peller, 1992). In working with adolescents, the concerned person can be a parent or guardian; another family member; a juvenile officer, school official, or social services agency representative; or a youth. Most often, a parent will schedule an appointment and come in with something he or she would like to see resolved with a son or daughter. On other occasions, a school official or juvenile officer will suggest, recommend, or mandate therapy for a youth.

It is necessary to make an important distinction at this point. Unlike pure problem- or solution-focused models, which suggest that the therapist should immediately search for "problems" or begin a quest for "solutions," a possibility therapy approach emphasizes the telling of each person's *story*. Why is this necessary? There are several reasons.

First, when a therapist initiates his or her own agenda from the start, without allowing an adolescent and others to relate their stories, it's as if the therapist is applying his or her model to the situation, regardless of the person or the circumstances. The uniqueness of the person becomes obsolete when a "one model fits all" mindset takes precedence. Erickson taught us that therapy ought to be client-driven, not theory-driven.

A second reason is given by A. Lawson, McElheran, and Slive (1997): "Research indicates that for many clients, the most valuable aspect of the therapy session is the opportunity to tell their story and be heard" (p. 15). As Carl Rogers (1951, 1961) taught us, people need to feel heard and understood. When a therapist attends mainly to his or her theory, and attempts to fit the client into its confines, the person may go unheard. If we did this in our everyday conversations, people would walk out on us or stop talking. After all, when you talk with others, do you ordinarily start to intervene with problem- or solution-loaded questions right from the start? Probably not. Do you let the person say what he or she needs to say? Probably. The idea here is that adolescents and others ought to have space for their stories to be told and heard.

There is a third reason that the telling of each person's story is crucial. If a person is cut off before having the space to relate his or her perspective, the therapist risks not learning about clients' understanding of the problem or their previous attempts to solve it. Clients can become disheartened when therapists suggest remedies that have already been unsuccessfully tried. By allowing each story to unfold, the therapist can attend to the remedies that have worked or failed for the adolescent and family.

This brings to light a myth about therapies that claim to be briefer than the standard treatment schedule. Brief therapies are often described as "shallow," which may be the case if they strive immediately for problem resolution or solution attainment. Possibility therapy begins with careful listening. Again, adolescents and others need to sense that they are being heard and understood. At the same time, there is no need to involve regression or the uncovering of pathology. Clients should have the opportunity to verbalize themselves in whatever way necessary, devoid of a therapist's theoretical interruptions.

To feel heard, people need not ramble on aimlessly or tell the entire story of their lives. In fact, as adolescents and their close relatives tell their stories, the therapist begins to do two things. First, openings can be introduced through collaborative, possibility-laced language. That is, the therapist can acknowledge and validate each person's experience and inject the element of possibility at the same time. Second, the therapist can help the narrators to gain a focus of what they would like to change. Before moving into how to do this, let's discuss possible opening questions.

Opening Things Up

Although there has been much debate over asking *the* right opening question, I suggest that the therapist remain fairly neutral at the start. This allows adolescents and their families to begin where they are most comfortable and let their stories unfold. Here are some possible opening questions for therapy (each requests slightly different information):

What has brought you in today?

Where would you like to begin?

What would you like to talk about?

Again, beginning with a neutral question and allowing an adolescent's, a parent's, or another person's story to evolve does not translate to aimless conversation. It invites people into a collaborative relationship where they can talk about whatever they feel most comfortable discussing, and about which they are most concerned. It can also be helpful with youth, who often expect to be blamed and lectured from the start. Furthermore, by opening with a neutral question, the therapist can catch a glimpse of how the person(s) communicates about his or her situation and life, and then begin to explore different ways of conversing and working in a more collaborative manner.

Carl Rogers with a Twist: Acknowledgment, Validation, and Possibility

When adolescents, parents, and others tell their stories, therapists need not remain stagnant or try to maintain constant neutrality. Instead, the therapist can begin to offer doorways with possibilities, through language. For this advice, we refer to Carl Rogers (1951, 1961), who taught us about the importance of empathy and acknowledgment in therapy.

Rogers related that, from the start, people need to feel heard and understood. If this does not happen, adolescents, in particular, will likely close down, become angry, or let the therapist know in some way that there is a problem. Parents will also let the therapist know that they are not being heard or that the therapist is not getting the message right. Thus, we must help people to feel heard and understood from the very beginning of therapy and *throughout the process*.

Still, as we listen and attend to adolescents and their families, if we only reflect back their experiences, these persons are unlikely to change. In fact, many will continue to box themselves into corners. They will describe situations that seem hopeless, with no way out. All the pure reflection in the world will not change that self-view.

What we want to do is add a twist to the idea of pure reflection (B. O'Hanlon, 1996c; B. O'Hanlon & Beadle, 1994; B. O'Hanlon & Bertolino, 1998). Many of the old Warner Brothers cartoons find the character "Roadrunner" trapped in a corner by "Wile E. Coyote." But just when it seems that Roadrunner is doomed, he seems to find a way out. One of the ways he does this (and he does it time and time again because it works for him!) is by painting a doorway with a knob on a wall near him, opening the door, and escaping. Through the use of language, we can do the same. We can help adolescents and families to move out of the corners they have talked themselves into by offering doorways with possibilities through language.

Here are three ways of doing this:

1. Reflect back clients' responses or problem reports in the past tense. Here are some examples of how to do this:

CLIENT: He's always in trouble.

THERAPIST: So he's been in trouble a lot.

CLIENT: I keep running away.

THERAPIST: You've run away many times.

CLIENT: I'm bad.

THERAPIST: You've felt bad about yourself.

When a youth, a parent, or another person involved in the therapy gives a present-tense statement of a problem, we acknowledge and reflect back the problem using the past tense. This is not pure Carl Rogers because we are moving beyond basic reflection. We are acknowledging and validating people where they are, and moving into the realm of possibilities at the same time.

As mentioned earlier, if we only acknowledge and validate, most adolescents may feel better but will still remain stuck. At the same time, if we only attempt to open up possibilities and do not acknowledge and validate, they may feel invalidated, blamed, and unheard. Thus, both pieces are necessary to the process—acknowledgment and possibility.

2. Take clients' general statements—"everything," "everybody," "nobody," "always," and "never"—and translate them into partial statements. This can be done by using qualifiers related to time (e.g., "recently," "in the last while," "in the past month or so," "most of the time," "much of the time"), intensity (e.g., "a bit less," "somewhat more"), or partiality (e.g., "a lot," "some," "most," "many"). We do not want to minimize the person's experience or invalidate his or her contribution. Instead, we want to gently introduce the idea of possibilities. Here are some examples:

CLIENT: I get in trouble all the time.

THERAPIST: So you get in trouble a lot of the time.

CLIENT: Nothing ever goes right for me.

THERAPIST: Sometimes it seems like nothing goes right.

CLIENT: I can't stop.

THERAPIST: Recently, you've been feeling like you can't stop.

The idea is to go from global statements to partial ones while continuing to acknowledge and validate the person. We want to create a little opening where change is possible.

3. Translate clients' statements of truth or reality—the way they explain things to themselves—into perceptual statements or subjective realities. Here are some ways to do this:

CLIENT: I'm a bad person because I'm always in trouble.

THERAPIST: So you've really gotten the idea that you are bad because you've been in trouble.

CLIENT: He'll never amount to anything.

THERAPIST: Because of what he's done, it seems to you that he'll never amount to anything.

CLIENT: I'm evil.

THERAPIST: Your sense is that there is evil in you.

Adolescents' and others' statements about adolescents are not the way things are, but the way they have perceived or experienced a particular thing. By reflecting back their statements as perceptions, we can introduce the notion of possibility.

When acknowledgment and validation are combined with language of change and possibility in ongoing therapist reflections, adolescents can begin to shift their self-perceptions. In addition, those who are associated with the youth can begin to alter their perceptions of them. We are speaking of a continuous process, throughout the therapy, whereby an adolescent or other person can come to a more possibility-oriented sense of self. The process becomes a part of the flow in therapy and helps to establish a context of change through constant acknowledgment. Possibilities open up through language.

If the therapist doesn't validate youth and others—if they feel minimized, or pushed to move on—the adolescents or others will react. They will say things like:

CLIENT: Not *most* of the time! *All* the time!

If the client reacts this way, we are not getting it right. We want to validate the client and introduce possibility.

THERAPIST: OK. Up to this point, you've been bad all the time.

This validates the perception while putting it in the past tense. These are subtle linguistic shifts—invitations rather than coercion or judgments. Youth have usually heard enough orders or judgments, which generally translate to invalidation and blame for them. We are not trying to dissuade anyone out of his or her perceptions and experiences. Instead, we want to offer the idea that even though the world has been difficult, change is possible.

By combining acknowledgment and validation with possibility, we can listen to the stories that are brought to therapy and simultaneously inject some hope into the situations being described. This is not magic, but it's like visiting a magic kingdom—there's something for everyone through the medium of language.

The following is a case example of how one can begin therapy and interject possibility-laced language:

Scott, a 14-year-old, was brought in for therapy by his mother after running away many times, stealing, and doing poorly in school. He had been able to avoid court involvement, but his mother had seemingly reached her end with him. Here is how the therapy began:

THERAPIST: Where would you like to begin?

MOTHER: I'm not sure. I mean, what hasn't Scott done? I can't trust him at all. He's run away something like eleven times. He just came back three days ago from being gone. He also stole from a convenience store—and that's just what I *know*. I can't help him. He won't listen to me or anyone. I can't imagine that this is going to help either, but I guess I have to at least try it.

THERAPIST: Sounds like a frustrating situation. He's done these things and it seems like you can't trust him and that he hasn't been listening to you. You've got the sense that nothing will help.

MOTHER: No doubt. Plus, there's school. He didn't pass last year and if he fails again—forget it. What am I supposed to do? You'd think that he'd see that if he continues to act this way he's gonna end up in some bad place. You know, like Boys' Town. I'm worried to death.

THERAPIST: Right, and you're worried because he's done some things that have led you to believe that he's heading for a big fall?

MOTHER: Right.

THERAPIST: And it seems like, because of what he's done, up until three days ago, that he's going to have to make some decision about where he wants to go with this? And maybe he's already done that, but it's unclear at this point.

MOTHER: Yeah.

THERAPIST: Scott, what's the scoop?

SCOTT: I just wanna hang out with my friends. It doesn't matter because she's just gonna get mad at something else even if I'm not late.

THERAPIST: OK, and you want to be with your friends and you feel like because she's been mad at you sometimes—because of your actions—if you come in early she might get mad at you about something else?

SCOTT: Yeah.

MOTHER: And that's really it. It's him being late. He can't just run the streets.

THERAPIST: You're worried about what he's been doing when he's been out and what could've happened to him.

MOTHER: Exactly.

Because the therapist opened with a neutral question, this mother was able to begin where she wished and tell her story. As she did, the therapist acknowledged her and simultaneously offered possibilities through subtle changes in language. The same was done with Scott. It is important that each person have the sense that he or she is being heard and understood, and that the problems are not static. This family's situation can change—and may have already (as evidenced by Scott's not running away for three days). These subtle offerings through language can inject the element of possibility into situations that appear to be closed down.

WHAT NEEDS TO CHANGE?

Creating a Focus

As we hear the stories that youth and their families bring to therapy, we want to begin to do two things: (a) introduce possibility-laced language into situations that seem to be closed down; and (b) create a focus by answering a couple of questions: What is the complaint? What needs to change? If we determine what the complaint is and what needs to change, we create a goal that is both achievable and solvable. Achievable goals consist of adolescents' actions, or conditions that can be brought about by their actions.

To determine what the complaint is, using *videotalk* can be very helpful (Hudson & O'Hanlon, 1991; B. O'Hanlon & Bertolino, 1998; B. O'Hanlon & Wilk, 1987). Videotalk involves getting adolescents and others to describe the problem as if it can be seen or heard on videotape. This means having clients use action-based language and describe how they "do" the problem. This way of conversing allows clients to move away from vague descriptions and non-sensory-based words and phrases about situations (e.g., "He's got a bad attitude," "She's out of control") toward concrete terms and solvable problems. For example, if a parent claims that his or her son has a "bad attitude," the therapist can inquire as to how the son *does* a bad attitude.

Here's one dialogue in which a therapist uses action-based language and videotalk to get a clear idea of a problem:

PARENT: My biggest concern is that Joseph has a bad attitude.

THERAPIST: So when Joseph is having a bad attitude, what specifically do you see him doing?

PARENT: He throws fits.

THERAPIST: OK. And if you were to videotape him having a bad attitude and I was to watch it, what would I see happening on that tape that would show me that he was throwing a fit?

PARENT: He would be throwing things around the room and cussing.

THERAPIST: Would he be throwing things at you too, or just around the room?

PARENT: Not at me. But he would be cussing at me.

THERAPIST: Is there anything else I would see him doing?

PARENT: He might be crying too.

By gaining an action-based or videotape description, the therapist can gain a clear picture of the complaint. Action-based language can also be helpful in translating psychiatric labels into process or action descriptions. The translation will assist the therapist and client in the creation of a solvable problem. Here's an example of how to do this:

PARENT: Jamie was diagnosed as ADHD [Attention Deficit Hyperactivity Disorder] last year, and the doctor told us that it never really goes away. It just changes as kids get older. So that's what's wrong. How do you deal with a kid who's ADHD? They just gave us some pamphlets and put her on medication.

THERAPIST: OK. It sounds like you've already done quite a bit to help your daughter. I'm not sure if you were told this or not, but there are lots of kids who have been diagnosed with ADHD and they do just fine. So what I'd like to find out from you is, what is it that Jamie is doing that seems to be a problem?

PARENT: Well, she doesn't do her homework.

THERAPIST: OK. So a lot of the time she's not getting her homework done. Is there anything else?

PARENT: Well, once in a while she talks back, but mainly it's her not getting her homework done that's a problem.

Another possibility would be to ask the parent: "How does your daughter *do* ADHD?" In either case, when labels are translated into action terms, the therapist can get a description of what is happening in behavioral terms. Anyone who has ever dealt with psychiatric labels knows that it's generally easier to work with an adolescent who is not doing his or her homework and is talking back than to globally work with a diagnosis such as ADHD.

Ironically, what people complain about is not always what they want to change. Some parents will have a complaint but will just want to be reassured that what their son or daughter is doing is "normal" or reasonable. They may just want to be heard and acknowledged. Thus, in gaining a focus, the therapist must make sure that the complaint is in fact what the family members want to see changed. With Scott, in the case discussed earlier, here's one way to gain a focus and make sure that the complaint is what the mother wants to change:

THERAPIST: So you're pretty frustrated because he's run away eleven times and was caught stealing?

MOTHER: Right. He's also failing all of his classes.

THERAPIST: OK. And you'd like to see all of these things take a turn for the better, because otherwise he might end up in placement. So, which of these things do you think is most important for us to focus on at this time?

MOTHER: The running away. I mean, the stealing was a year ago, so I'm not as worried about it as I am the running away. He knows that if he continues taking off he's gonna get locked up real fast.

THERAPIST: I see. You're most worried about his runaways because that seems to be the fastest track to placement.

MOTHER: Right.

THERAPIST (TO THE YOUTH): Scott, what do you think about that?

SCOTT: I don't want to get locked up.

THERAPIST: How come?

SCOTT: Because then I wouldn't be able to do anything.

THERAPIST: OK. Do you agree with your mom about the running away, or do you think we should be talking about other stuff?

SCOTT: I know I can't run away but that's not really what I'm doing. I'm just with my friends.

THERAPIST: If you're with your friends when you don't have permission, or after curfew, what would you call that?

SCOTT: I guess it's a runaway—but I come back.

THERAPIST: You do come back and I can see that your mom is glad that nothing has happened to you. Does it make sense that she's worried that something could happen to you and you may be locked up because you're with your friends when you're not supposed to be?

SCOTT: Yeah. I know I've got to stop.

THERAPIST: Is that reasonable for her to want to have you around?

SCOTT: Yeah.

The therapist's job is to work collaboratively with the adolescent, family members, and others who have a voice in the therapy (i.e., juvenile officers, teachers, and so on), to negotiate realistic and achievable goals. In most cases, there will be a different agenda and at least one complaint for each person. For instance, a mother's goal may be for her daughter to stop skipping school. A daughter's goal may be to get her mother off her back. According to S. O'Hanlon and O'Hanlon (1997), when there are multiple complaints, "We try to acknowledge and address each complaint and combine them into mutual complaints and goals on which to focus our inquiries and interventions" (p. 5).

Acknowledgment, tracking, and linking are commonly used to coordinate complaints and goals. First, each person's position is acknowledged and restated in the least inflammatory way possible, while still acknowledging and imparting the intended feeling and meaning (S. O'Hanlon & O'Hanlon, 1997). These statements are then linked together with the word "and." This builds a common concern and a mutual goal. In the situation described above, here's how a therapist might coconstruct a mutual goal with the mother and daughter:

CAROL (MOTHER): I just want her to return to school. This is ridiculous for her to be out.

THERAPIST: OK. You can't really see any reason why she shouldn't be in school.

CAROL: Right.

LESLIE (DAUGHTER): What's the point? I can't stand it. Besides, if you're gonna continue to be on my case, then I'll never go back.

THERAPIST: And Leslie, you feel like there's little reason to go to school.

LESLIE: Yeah.

THERAPIST: Let me see if I've got this straight. Please let me know if I'm off base here. Carol, you'd like your daughter to return to school and see her get an education and have an easier time reaching her dreams. And Leslie, you'd like to get your mother off your back and get some space and move on to getting to where you want to be with your life.

If we are off base, the family members will let us know. They will jump in and clarify any misperceptions until a mutually agreeable description emerges. Once the therapist is clear on this, a goal can be created via action or videotalk.

The Magical World of Motivation

As discussed earlier, everyone is motivated for something. Adolescents are motivated either toward a desired experience or goal (e.g., money, freedom) or away from an unpleasant or unwanted experience (e.g., boredom, restrictions). Michael Durrant (1993) remarked, "When young people appear to be unmotivated, it is often the goals that are the problem" (p. 64). In working with adolescents, it is crucial that they have a say in whatever goals are established. To ensure that a youth feels that a goal is just, he or she should be asked. For example, I frequently say things such as, "Will that work for you?" Or, "What do you think about that goal?"

If a goal is not agreeable to any one party, it is up to the therapist to backtrack and become more of a negotiator, as in the following case example:

Lucy was mandated to therapy for stealing from a department store. Her mother was vehement about Lucy's not going into any store without her, fearing that Lucy might steal again. In addition, the mother did not want Lucy to hang out with the friends with whom she had been caught stealing. Initially, Lucy agreed with this, but as the first session came to a close, she made it clear that she was dissatisfied. Lucy remarked, "She's getting what she wants, but all I get is in trouble. Why should I even try? She still won't let me do anything!" The therapist replied, "I can see that this seems very unfair to you, and it may be. I'm not sure. But the first thing is: Should you decide to not try, that's up to you. You're capable of making that decision for yourself. So you're still responsible for what you decide to do or, in this situation, decide not to do. OK? Now, how can you let your mother know that you don't feel like this is a fair goal?" Lucy proceeded to approach her mother in a respectful way and, after some further negotiation, a more amicable goal was agreed on.

HOW WILL YOU KNOW WHEN IT'S BETTER?

After it becomes clear what the adolescent and family want to change, the next step is to inquire: What will that change look like when it happens? The question can be asked of each person involved in the therapy. When they reply, have the participants use action-based talk. What will the youth and/or other members of the family be doing when things are better?

Videotalk

The use of videotalk can be helpful at this juncture. This way of conversing will allow people to move away from vague descriptions (e.g., "He'll be good;" "She'll be calmer;" "He won't be acting bad") of what change will look like when it happens. Videotalk is especially useful with adolescents because it asks others to outline their expectations in concrete terms. Here is a general way of asking for a videotape description:

THERAPIST: Let's say that a few weeks, months, or more time, has elapsed and the problem you came here for has been resolved. If we were to watch a videotape of your son/daughter/family in the future, what would he/she/they be doing on that tape that would show that things *are* better?

Another way to find out what it will be like when things are better is to use action talk. Here is an example:

THERAPIST: When you feel that your daughter has turned the corner and is doing better, what will she be doing?

PARENT: Well, she'll stop acting strange.

THERAPIST: OK. Now I'm kind of unclear about what that will look like. Can you be more specific about what she'll be doing when she's no longer acting strange?

PARENT: Well, she won't be running away.

THERAPIST: All right. Anything else?

PARENT: Yeah. She won't be bugging me all the time.

THERAPIST: When she bugs you, how does she do it?

PARENT: She just gets on my nerves.

THERAPIST: I sometimes get bugged when people talk at movies. Is it like that or different?

PARENT: She interrupts me by calling me at my office over and over for no reason because she's not getting her way.

THERAPIST: OK, so when things have turned the corner she won't be calling you at your office over and over. If she does call, it will be for a good reason. What would be a good reason? Does she know?

PARENT: If there's a crisis or she needs permission to do something, but if I've told her "No," calling me over and over is only going to make me more mad. It's not going to change anything.

THERAPIST: So she'll be more respectful about when and when not to call you, and she'll take "No" as an answer more often?

PARENT: Right.

Action language helps to clarify people's expectations in behavioral terms. For youth, this can make a difference; they can get a clearer understanding of what is expected of them. If people seem to struggle with generating what the future will look like in action terms, it can be helpful to give examples, as I did in the above sequence. Multiple-choice questions are also a way of helping people to clarify what they will see happening. For example, a therapist could say, "Will she be doing _____ or _____ or _____ ?" The person can either select one of the choices or come up with a different description altogether.

Scaling Questions

Some therapists prefer to use questions that indicate incremental or quantitative change. A popular method involves the use of scaling questions (Berg & de Shazer, 1993; Berg & Miller, 1992;

de Shazer, 1991, 1994; Lipchik, 1988). Although there are variations of this technique, the therapist usually begins by describing a scale of one to ten where each number represents a rating of the client's complaint on a continuum. Here's an example of how scaling questions might be used with adolescents and families:

THERAPIST: On a scale of one to ten, with one being the worst this problem has ever been, and ten being the best things could ever be, where would you rate things today?

Once the therapist is given a number, he or she explores how that rating translates into action talk. For example, if a parent rates things at a two, the therapist asks for a description of what constitutes a two. Then, he or she inquires as to where things would need to be for the parent to feel that the goals of therapy were met. If the same parent says that an eight would indicate sufficient change, the therapist would ask for a description of what will be happening when things are rated eight.

With scaling questions, and in the general effort to determine what is better, it's important that the therapist work with the youth, family members, or others to identify "in-between" changes. For example, if a parent describes things as being at a two and is striving for an eight, it is essential that the therapist help the family to identify what will represent change between two and eight. In working with adolescents, it's generally helpful to identify small changes. A therapist might ask, "If things are at a one now, what would it take to get to a two and a half?" It's up to the therapist to work with the family to determine when a goal is too big a leap.

Percentage Questions

Similar to scaling questions are questions that ask for percentages of change. To use this method, the therapist first finds out what percentage of the time things are going well or are manageable, from the perspective of the adolescent, parent, or other person. The therapist then asks, "What percentage of the time would things need to be going well or manageable, for you to feel that therapy was successful?" Again, it is important that the therapist is clear on what will constitute in-between change.

Attending to Differences: Clarifying Outcomes

As with establishing goals, all parties will not always agree on what constitutes "better" or a successful outcome. For instance, a father may want to see his daughter improve in all her classes at once. Meanwhile, the mother may feel that therapy will be successful when her daughter improves her grades in two classes. Most of the time, further negotiation will help the therapist to gain clarification. In the event that there is still some disagreement, determining who initiated the therapy and who has the ability to terminate it can clear up the differences. Table 2.3 offers questions that will help therapists to gain clarity in the event that there seems to be an impasse.

TABLE 2.3
CLARIFYING WHAT CONSTITUTES SUCCESSFUL THERAPY

❖ What is bothering this group enough to get them to seek or get sent to treatment?

❖ Who is complaining?

❖ Who is alarmed about something?

❖ What are they complaining or alarmed about? (Translate vague and blaming words into action descriptions—use action/videotalk.)

❖ Who is willing to pay for therapy and/or do something to effect change?

❖ Whose concerns will constrain or affect therapy?

❖ Who is pushing for change?

❖ Who is paying the therapy bill?

❖ Who is complaining the most?

❖ Who will be able to terminate therapy?

❖ What are the legal and ethical restraints or considerations (suicidal plans/attempts, homicidal and violence plans/history, court/legal involvement, and so on)?

ROLLER COASTER AND RIVERBOAT RIDES

Striving for What's Manageable

A woman brought her 15-year-old daughter and 12-year-old son to therapy because, late one night, they had taken her car for a "joy ride." During their excursion, they ran into another vehicle and then abandoned the car. According to the woman, her children had also been involved in stealing and were "constantly in trouble."

"It's all too much. I feel like I'm on a roller coaster," she explained.

I inquired, "If you could get off the roller coaster and change rides, what would you choose?"

"Well, I've never liked roller coasters. I prefer the calm rides—maybe a riverboat ride."

"How might a riverboat ride be different from a roller coaster?"

She said, "Roller coasters move too fast and they go up and down too much. There's just too many hills and dips. Riverboat rides can be bumpy, but not too bumpy, and they're slower."

To this woman, a riverboat ride was symbolic of a calmer, more workable situation. She didn't mind a few bumps because that's what life is like. However, life on a roller coaster was too much for her. Interestingly, when parents or others are asked to describe what their lives will look like when things are better, most will not strive for perfection. They will not say things like "We won't have any more problems," or "Life will be like The Brady Bunch." Instead, it's more common for people to describe situations that are simply more manageable.

In the 1996 movie, *Shine,* David Helfgott (played by Geoffrey Rush) is portrayed as struggling with mental illness apparently associated with the traumatic events of his childhood. Near the end of the film, he is shown performing on a piano in front of a large audience, and it is clear that he has made incredible strides. Most people cheered this outcome and his overall accomplishments, but some criticized the movie because he was not "better"—there were still remnants of mental illness present (i.e., rapid speech, scattered thoughts, odd behavior, and so on).

Those who made the critical comments entirely missed the point. David Helfgott went from a roller coaster to a riverboat ride. His life was greatly improved; he could function much better than he previously did. That was part of the triumph. The goal had not been to go from mental illness to no symptoms at all.

This realism also seems to be present among difficult adolescents and their families. Most families simply want improvement and some relief; they do not expect a problem-free lifestyle. They will not seek perfection. When we can keep this in mind, and help families to move from peaks and valleys to a landscape that has only some bumps in its terrain, change can become much more attainable.

Most often, the changes that people desire will be reasonable. However, once in a while, a parent will be so frustrated or exhausted with a youth or a situation that he or she will express a desire for changes that are unreasonable or unattainable. Here is an example of how to work with such a situation:

THERAPIST: So you're most concerned about Jordan fighting with his sister?

MOTHER: That's just the tip of the iceberg! All the crap he's doing needs to stop now. He needs to pull it together now and behave. That includes not fighting, doing his homework, coming in on time, doing what I tell him without talking back. . . . Whatever I say, he just needs to do it.

THERAPIST: This seems pretty frustrating to you.

MOTHER: It is—very.

THERAPIST: And it feels like, to you, that if he makes those changes right away, things might be better?

MOTHER: Exactly.

THERAPIST: I can see how that might make things better. Now, you have three other children. Based on your experiences with raising them, what do you think the chances are that all those things you talked about will change with Jordan right away? Great? Average? Not so good?

MOTHER: Well, my other kids didn't do all those things. They did other things.

THERAPIST: Right, what they did was probably different. But what does your experience tell you?

MOTHER: I guess that he probably won't change everything overnight.

THERAPIST: OK. Everything could change overnight; that's possible. But if that doesn't happen, what do you think is the most important thing that needs to change first?

MOTHER: I guess the fighting. I can't stand that.

THERAPIST: OK. So you'd like to see all the things you talked about before change, and quickly if possible; but given your experience with raising kids, it seems that all those things changing at once might be a stretch. So if we kept an eye on all your concerns but focused mostly on the fighting right now, would that fit your needs?

MOTHER: Yep.

This particular woman was frustrated. What I did was acknowledge her position and then move on to creating a goal that was achievable and attainable in her eyes. It is important to first help people to feel heard or understood. The therapist can then begin to use possibility language and the experiences of others to move toward more realistic goals. It is my experience that, most of the time, unrealistic expectations represent frustration, anxiety, or some internal experience. Thus, validating clients' internal experiences before modifying the goal can diffuse these situations.

KEEPING THE LINES MOVING

If you've ever been to Disneyland or Walt Disney World, it's likely that you experienced an interesting phenomenon and don't even know it. Although the lines are long and it may take an hour or even two to get on a ride, they seem to keep moving (Efran & Lukens, 1985). Rarely do you stand still for very long. In addition, on many of the rides, the entertainment begins once you get in line. There are televisions with videos playing, or things to look at along the way. The line would take just as long if you were standing still, but because you are moving, you get the sense that you are making progress toward your end goal.

When working with adolescents and their families, we can use a similar premise. The following case example illustrates this point:

Michelle was brought in by her mother after refusing to go to school for two months. At the start of therapy, the mother was asked, "When things are going the way you want, what will be happening?" She stated that her daughter would be going to school and "feeling good about herself." Because the latter part was vague, she was asked what Michelle will be doing when she is "feeling good about herself." She related that her daughter will be smiling and going out with her friends more often. Michelle was also asked what "better" might look like for her. She stated that she will be going to school and will have a job she liked. Once it was clear what "better" will be like, the mother and daughter were asked what signs they will be looking for, to tell them that things are heading in the direction that they outlined. They both said that things will begin "one day at a time," starting with Michelle's returning to school for one day, and her "smiling" at least two times a day. After they left the session, Michelle attended four straight days before missing again. Further, her mother commented that she had seen Michelle smile "too many times to count." After two more sessions, she was going to school regularly.

The change this family desired could have happened in one session or fifty sessions. Regardless of the time frame needed for change, when the mother saw Michelle return to school for even a day, and then smile, she sensed that things were moving forward. These were signs of improvement, but it's likely that neither Michelle nor her mom would have seen the progress if the therapist hadn't helped them to notice what was happening. By using collaborative, possibility-laced language as the medium, we can help clients to begin to become unstuck. By noticing what's going on around them, they see that they are moving toward their designated goals.

The next chapter discusses how adolescents' and others' views of problems and complaints can be changed, leading to problem resolution.

CHAPTER THREE

The Lost Worldview

EVOKING NEW POSSIBILITIES
IN THE REALM OF VIEWING

*What an immeasurable honor . . . witnessing firsthand
your understanding of the human spirit. Your work is
truly your love made visible.*

—Actor Djimon Honsou in a letter
to director Steven Spielberg, describing
his experience with the director
during the making of *Amistad*

*W*HEN *STEVEN SPIELBERG WAS a teenager and living in Phoenix, he was a member of the Flaming Arrow Patrol of Ingleside's Troop 294. One of the parents who supervised the boys during this time was a man named Dick Hoffman. Over time, as people do, Hoffman developed an image of the young Spielberg. He described his view of Steven:*

> *He seemed to go in fits and starts—he would dash from one thing to another. I thought it was a disability, not being able to concentrate the way the rest of us would. I knew he was wildly enthusiastic, but I didn't think he had enough ability to analyze things. . . . I thought, "When he grows up and gets into the real world he's going to have a tough time keeping up." I didn't dream anything would come of him. Of course, that was a complete misjudgment of the kid's personality. (McBride, 1997, pp. 77–78)*

The views that youth hold about themselves, or that others hold about them, relate to what is being noticed in their lives. Views can be in the form of *attentional patterns* and *stories*. With attentional patterns, parents, youth, or others typically focus on certain aspects of an adolescent or his or her life. As mentioned in Chapter 1, stories represent how youth or others have come to describe their perceptions.

The views that clients subscribe to can engender hope or close down possibilities. Often, when troubling problems develop with adolescents and families, it's because unhelpful attentional patterns and/or stories have developed. This chapter offers ways of helping to change unhelpful views that youth have of themselves, as well as those that others have about them.

To get a clearer picture of the role that views play, I'll discuss the realm of stories and then move on to attentional patterns.

FROM EXPERIENCE TO STORIES

People develop their perspectives based on who they are, including their past experiences and social interactions. As discussed in Chapter 2, what adolescents experience internally is all OK and should be acknowledged and validated; however, the stories that youth, as well as others, subscribe to may be unhelpful at times. Thus, stories that are hopeful and leave open possibilities for change should be promoted, and those that close down avenues of change should be challenged. White and Epston (1990) have referred to stories that close down possibilities as being *problem saturated;* that is, when problem saturated or problematic stories about youth are present, the possibilities of change can seem virtually nonexistent.

The views about youth that youth and others abide by are subject to negotiation and change. They aren't set in stone. When these stories already hold the possibility of change, we can work with youth so they can take *action* to make them happen. In contrast, when stories are problematic or closed down, we must first help to negotiate new ways of viewing that are conducive to change. How can we recognize stories that are problematic? Let's find out.

Four Kinds of Problematic Stories

As mentioned, when youth are experiencing trouble, frequently they will hold stories about themselves that close down the possibilities for change. More often, family members, friends or acquaintances, teachers, juvenile officers, or others will also subscribe to stories about youth that are restrictive or closed down. These stories are unhelpful when they get in the way of change. There are four kinds of problematic stories (B. O'Hanlon, 1996d; B. O'Hanlon & Bertolino, 1998): stories of *impossibility, blame, invalidation,* and *nonaccountability.*

1. STORIES OF IMPOSSIBILITY

In stories of *impossibility,* youth or therapists hold ideas that suggest that change with a youth or a situation is impossible. When people abide by such stories, they will often say things such as, "He'll (I'll) never change," "He's (I'm) conduct-disordered; don't expect much," or "She's (I've) always been that way and always will be."

A 14-year-old female was referred for "chronic truancy." She had missed over ninety days during the school year. On the referral form, a school counselor had written, "This adolescent has had a history of truancy since the age of 10. Given the chronic and ongoing nature of this problem, it is extremely unlikely that she will change her behavior anytime soon."

2. Stories of Blame

A second type of problematic stories are those that *blame*. With these stories, youth or therapists blame youth for bad intentions or bad traits. It is suggested that an adolescent's bad intentions are purposeful, intentional, or preconceived. When stories of blame are being played out, youth or others will say things such as, "She has no intention of changing," "He's always playing head games and never serious about anything," or "I guess I do act out to get my mom's attention."

A man brought his son to therapy after discovering that he had left home at 2:00 A.M. to go partying with his friends. The man said, "He doesn't have a clue what's important! He's just like his mother, always trying to piss me off and give me a heart attack."

3. Stories of Invalidation

Stories of *invalidation* are the third kind of problematic story. These types of stories are related to ideas that lead to an adolescent's personal experience or knowledge being undermined by others—parents, family members, mental health professionals, or any person who is involved in the individual's personal life. Statements associated with stories of invalidation might include, "You shouldn't feel that way," "Just let it go," or "You must pass through five stages to fully resolve your problem."

A single mother came to therapy with her adolescent son. The woman remarked, "Lots of kids have fathers who aren't involved in their lives, so why doesn't he just get over it? It's not worth getting that upset over."

4. STORIES OF NONACCOUNTABILITY

The final type of stories that often show up with youth are stories of *nonaccountability*—nonchoice or determinism. In these cases, it is suggested that a youth has no choice about what he or she does voluntarily; that is, the adolescent is said to have no ability or control to make any difference in what happens in his or her life. The distinction here is that what youth do voluntarily with their bodies, they are accountable for and have choice in. This is different from what others do to them and their bodies, in which they do not have a choice. Here is an example that shows this distinction:

A young woman was attending a party with some friends. During the evening, she became intoxicated and started a fight with another girl. She thought the girl was trying to take away her boyfriend. Later that evening, as she was returning home, she was raped by a male who had been at the same party.

The young woman was accountable for what she did with her body and for those areas where she had choices—drinking alcohol and getting into a fight. She was not accountable for what was done to her that she had no choice in—being raped.

When youth are subscribing to stories of nonchoice or determinism, they will sometimes say things like "He started it," "If she would leave me alone, I wouldn't hit her," or "It's just the way my family taught me, so it's all I know. You know, an eye for an eye."

A therapist from a youth agency presented a seminar on how to work with "aggressive youth." During the initial part of her presentation, she remarked, "Research shows that youth who were abused by their parent or parents will 'naturally' be aggressive toward others who remind them of their parents."

A common thread among these four problematic stories is that they all create a mirage or smokescreen for therapists. Problematic stories are deceiving in that they appear to be so real that therapists can become entranced by them. Therapists can become convinced that what they are observing is the truth. We want to recognize that what actually exists behind these mirages is an adolescent who is bigger than any one story or narrative. Instead of becoming participants in the four types of problematic stories about youth, we want to challenge or cast doubt on them. Our task is to open up possibilities where there don't seem to be any.

Problematic Attentional Patterns

A major league baseball player was having an "all-star" season. He was leading the league in hitting and playing better than he ever had. After the midseason All-Star Game break, he returned to the diamond only to find that he was struggling as a hitter. He couldn't believe that things had changed so quickly. When he continued to slump at the plate, he decided to go back and watch videotape footage of himself hitting, in an effort to find out what he was doing wrong. As the player watched tapes of himself striking out and hitting weak ground balls, he noticed that he was pulling off pitches. He also noticed that he was lunging at the ball, and he was moving his feet too much. Soon, he was more down than before he had watched the tapes, knowing that he had so many things to correct in his batting. As he continued to study the videotapes, the team's hitting coach, who was wandering through the corridor, spotted the player.

The coach inquired, "What are you doing?"

"I'm watching tapes of myself to figure out what I'm doing wrong," explained the player.

The coach followed with, "Why are you watching yourself strike out and do poorly? You ought to be watching tapes of yourself that show you playing the way that you're capable of. Watch the ones that show you hitting the ball hard and doing the things you want to do at the plate."

The player said that he hadn't thought of that before and did as the coach had suggested.

Within a few short games, he had his swing back and was on track with his hitting again.

Problems in the realm of viewing come in two circumstances: (a) when problematic stories are held, and (b) when adolescents or others have unhelpful attentional patterns—that is, when an adolescent or other person is utilizing a restricted frame of reference.

The baseball player was not holding a "wrong" view, just an unhelpful one. The coach merely suggested that he should attend to his concern in a different way. Once the player followed suit, he was able to gain a new perspective that ultimately contributed to the improvement in his hitting. W. O'Hanlon and Weiner-Davis (1989) commented that a shift in view "can lead to changes in action and the stimulation of unused potentials and resources" (p. 126). This can be especially helpful with adolescents and families. Often, a small shift in a pattern of attention can lead to a significant change in how a person or situation is dealt with.

CHANGING PROBLEMATIC STORIES AND PATTERNS OF VIEWING

When adolescents or others hold problematic stories or attentional patterns, it can be difficult for them to see things from another perspective. Thus, our task is to help adolescents, family members, and others to change the unhelpful views to which they subscribe. Again, this requires the therapist to consider, "What else?" That question can lead to a shift in attention or to the creation of a new story that engenders hope and possibility.

A couple and their twin 12-year-old daughters came to therapy because the girls were "constantly fighting" with one another. According to the parents, some of the fights had been serious—twice, one of the girls had been taken to a hospital emergency room for medical attention. The father commented, "Everyone knows that twins are very close" and "When people are that close, sometimes they fight." Both parents held the view that because their daughters were twins and were "naturally" very close, the fighting was something that was to be expected.

The parents were asked what else they knew about twins, and it turned out that they were well read on the topic. Next, they were asked, "What does the literature say about twins and random fighting?" The couple could only repeat that closeness could lead to some fighting. The therapist offered, "I understand that your daughters are close and that's a possible factor. But not all twins that are close fight. So I'm curious, what else do you think may contribute to their fighting and how come it's only once a week?" The parents were unsure, so it was suggested that they go home and notice what may be contributing to the situation.

The next week, the parents came in and reported that the girls attend a school where the classes rotate. For instance, their last class on Monday is their first on Tuesday, and their third class on Thursday becomes their fourth on Friday. The girls had one class together—gym. It was held twice a week, coming in the middle of the day once a week and as the last class of the day once a week. When gym was in the middle of the day, the girls would go to different classes and continue with their schedules without incident. However, when gym was the last class of the day, they would come home with a fury and go after one another because they had not had a chance to "wind down."

The parents stated, "We just need to know each week which day they have gym together and then we can be prepared for them when they come home." They were asked, "What about random fighting between people who are close?" The father replied, "I think everyone fights randomly. But with the girls it's a matter of them winding down."

It is common for parents and those close to adolescents to tune into one or two aspects of youth or their situation, because those aspects are most noticeable or alarming. From these views, generalizations and problematic stories can be created, and these may contribute to the stuckness that's being experienced. By helping people to shift attention elsewhere, unhelpful views can be changed. In the twins' case, a small shift in the viewing can lead to changes in action and behavior. The parents' shift in attention led to new action in dealing with the girls.

Next, let's explore three ways to challenge or cast doubt on problematic stories and unhelpful patterns of attention: by transforming the story, finding counterevidence, or finding alternatives that fit the same facts.

Transform the Story by Acknowledging and Adding the Element of Possibility

The previous chapter offered ways of acknowledging adolescents' and others' experiences while simultaneously opening up possibilities. Acknowledgment of current or past problematic points of view, combined with the element of possibility, can help to reorient people to different parts or aspects of their lives or situations. Here's an example of how to do this:

PARENT: Clearly, he only thinks about himself. He doesn't care about anyone else.

THERAPIST: A lot of what he's been doing has given you the idea that he only cares about himself.

PARENT: Yeah. He hasn't shown me any differently. It's frustrating.

THERAPIST: Based on what you've seen, up until now it seems he hasn't shown you any differently, and that's been frustrating.

PARENT: That's right. I'm waiting, but it's frustrating.

By acknowledging this parent's internal experience (frustration) and then introducing the possibility that change may occur by using statements relating to partiality ("A lot"), perceptions ("has given you the idea"), and past tense ("been doing," "you've seen," and "hasn't shown"), the problematic view began to be deconstructed and transformed. Within a few moments, this parent went from "he only thinks about himself" to "I'm waiting." This represents a shift in view from believing that the son only thinks of himself to the possibility that, at some time, he will show up differently in the eyes of his parent.

Find Counterevidence

The goal here is to have the adolescent, parent, or other person tell you something that doesn't fit with the problematic story. Again, this involves asking, "What else?" To find counterevidence, the therapist acknowledges all internal experience of those in therapy, and then explores other aspects of a person's life, event, or situation. Here's an example of how counterevidence can play a role in the shifting of views:

FATHER: Dana never goes by the rules. In fact, I don't know why we even have rules. They don't do any good with her.

THERAPIST: Your sense is that Dana isn't into rules. What rules in particular that she's broken have been most bothersome to you?

FATHER: Well, the not-doing-her-chores thing, for one. I can't get her to lift a finger.

THERAPIST: OK. It seems that she hasn't helped out as much as she is capable of. When was the last time you can remember her pitching in?

FATHER: I don't know. Maybe a month ago she helped her mother out with the dishes.

DANA: Uh uh! I did the dishes all by myself yesterday!

FATHER: Wow! Wonders never cease! You should have done them.

THERAPIST: Was that a fluke? Or do you sometimes do other things too?

DANA: My room is always clean and I take the dog out every morning and after school.

THERAPIST (TO THE FATHER): Is this accurate?

FATHER: She does do that stuff, but she's supposed to.

THERAPIST: Right. There are some responsibilities she has and it's been frustrating to you when she doesn't do them all. Is it safe to say that some rules she does better with than others?

FATHER: Yeah. That's true.

The problematic story and view presented by the father was that Dana "never" went by the rules. What I did was acknowledge his concern while introducing possibility language, including statements to reflect perceptions ("Your sense is"), past tense ("hasn't helped"), and partiality ("as much"). Then, I began to explore for counterevidence that might dispute the problematic story and lead to a change in the viewing.

To find counterevidence, I usually begin in the present and work my way backward. My reason: The more current the evidence, the stronger it will be. Sometimes, a therapist may have to go back a few months, a year, or even a few years, to find evidence that contradicts the problem story. That's OK. Evidence is evidence. It's easier to evoke or elicit past abilities and competencies than to teach someone something he or she has never done. For example, if an adolescent is trying to resolve a conflict (which nearly everyone has done at one time or another), it's much easier to find a time when he or she was successful in this area in the past, and explore and build on that, than to teach "conflict resolution" or "anger management," or do "assertiveness training."

In addition, when therapists only teach skills such as those just mentioned, family members may only turn to "experts" when future problems arise. The family will downplay or mistrust the significance of their own unique solutions and perspectives (Nylund & Corsiglia, 1994; C. Smith, 1997; Zimmerman & Dickerson, 1996). Thus, searching for counterevidence relies on evoking and eliciting competency rather than giving an adolescent, a parent, or another person a tool that may or may not work, may or may not be used, and does not involve personal experiences such as abilities, strengths, resources, and solutions (past, present, or future).

Find Alternative Stories or Frames That Fit the Same Evidence or Facts

Sometimes, when an adolescent's or other person's interpretation of another person, event, or situation is closed down, a therapist's interpretation can offer a different point of view and lead to the dissolution of a problematic story. Specifically, when an adolescent or other person makes a closed-down statement relating to a problematic story, the therapist can *offer* an alternative story or interpretation. Here are a couple of examples:

ADOLESCENT: My parents don't have a clue how to raise me. All they do is ground me and make my life miserable.

THERAPIST: It seems to you that their mission is to put restrictions on you and make your life miserable. You know, your parents haven't raised a 16-year-old before, and you haven't been a 16-year-old before. I wonder if maybe your parents are doing what they think is best, and you just haven't educated them about what it's like to be a 16-year-old in the 1990s.

PARENT: I tried to teach her well but it hasn't worked. Tracy just continues to fight with me.

THERAPIST: It seems to you that your efforts to teach her haven't been as successful as you'd like. You know, you mentioned that some things come quicker than others for you, and I have to wonder if maybe she's just learning at her own pace too. She's learned other things from you and it sounds like maybe she just hasn't picked up on this one yet.

Again, it is important to use acknowledgment and possibility-laced language in conjunction with an interpretation. In addition, the therapist introduces any interpretation from a position of *conjecture* or wonderment (Andersen, 1991; Hoffman, 1990; Penn & Sheinberg, 1991). This is done by prefacing questions with sentence stems such as "I wonder," "Is it possible," or "Could it be." Conjecture allows the therapist to offer alternative views from a position of curiosity as opposed to stating them as truths or facts.

CREATING COMPELLING FUTURES WITH POSSIBILITIES

The Moving Walkway: From Problem to Possibility

As mentioned in the previous chapter, youth and family members often find themselves in corners merely because of the way their situations are described or *languaged*. In turn, the way that we talk with them can have a significant influence on the stories that evolve. In Chapter 2, we discussed some ways of introducing the element of possibility through dialoguing. We learned how to paint doorways in corners with language and in some way subtly introduce possibilities into an otherwise closed-down view. Possibility-laced language provides a skeleton key for these situations.

We can begin to open up possibilities for change through language by using the principle employed in a "moving walkway" (B. O'Hanlon, 1996c; B. O'Hanlon & Bertolino, 1998). At airports, moving conveyor belts carry people toward their personal destinations; our use of language can do the same. Youth, parents, juvenile officers, teachers, and others may come to us with views and stories that are without possibilities, but there are ways of interviewing, asking questions, making comments, and telling stories that can create an effect similar to that of a moving walkway (B. O'Hanlon & Bertolino, 1998). By using language as a conveyor belt, we can help youth to create a compelling sense of a personal destination—a future with possibilities—before they even take any action. Just as moving walkways require little effort in transporting people, we can help youth to move toward their future possibilities without any conscious effort on their part. There are three ways of doing this:

1. Assume the possibility of youth, families, and associated parties finding solutions; use words such as "yet" and "so far." These words presuppose that even though things feel stuck or unchangeable in the present, things will change sometime in the future. This simple shift in language can help to create a "light at the end of the tunnel."

   CLIENT: He'll never amount to anything.

   THERAPIST: So far you haven't seen any evidence that he'll change.

   CLIENT: I'm always in trouble.

   THERAPIST: You haven't found a way to stay out of trouble yet.

   CLIENT: I don't have a future. Why should I even try?

   THERAPIST: Up to this point you haven't found a reason to try and make things better in your life.

2. Recast the problem statement into a statement about the preferred future or goal.

   CLIENT: I'll never get out of the gang.

   THERAPIST: So you'd like to be able to find a way to get out of the gang?

   CLIENT: No one cares what happens to me.

   THERAPIST: So you'd like to know that people care about you?

   CLIENT: I've been in trouble all of my life.

   THERAPIST: So one of the things that we could do in here is help you to find a way to change your relationship with trouble?

3. Presuppose that changes and progress toward goals will occur by using words like "when" and "will."

CLIENT: No one wants to hang out with me because all I do is get into trouble.

THERAPIST: So when you start to get friends, how do you think you'll act differently than before?

CLIENT: I can't stop. All I know how to do is get in trouble.

THERAPIST: So when you've put trouble behind you, what will you be doing?

CLIENT: All people do is blame me.

THERAPIST: When you're no longer feeling blamed, how will things be different?

By using the moving walkway to introduce possibilities through language, therapists can begin to create openings where walls seemed to previously exist. This way of talking with youth and families is an ongoing process; it allows clinicians to continue to open pathways during the course of therapy. By using possibility language such as the words associated with the moving walkway, we can begin to introduce the idea of change by challenging and casting doubt on problematic stories and attentional patterns.

BACK TO THE FUTURE: COCREATING PREFERRED FUTURES

Upon entering therapy, youth often present themselves as having no view or vision of the future. In addition, other mental health professionals, family members, teachers, and juvenile officers will sometimes convey the idea that a youth is incapable of change, or perhaps has no future. After hearing such a story from a respected professional, it can seem that an adolescent really is doomed.

How can we avoid being persuaded by these types of stories? One way is by helping youth cocreate a sense of a preferred future—a future where things work out, a problem is resolved, or a goal is reached. Notice that I am using the term *cocreate* as opposed to just *create*. As discussed earlier, therapy is a collaborative effort that is informed by language. Through the medium of language, preferred futures are negotiated among the therapist, youth, family members, and other collaborators. Ultimately, the preferred future will be the youth's, but, through interaction to construct the idea, the therapist contributes to the process.

It is common for us to think of the past as causing the present, and the present as causing the future. In fact, we often live our lives by this adage and say to youth, "That will affect your future." But let's think about this a little differently for a moment. In the movie *Back to the Future II,* Marty McFly (played by Michael J. Fox) continually finds himself in situations where his behavior in the future will have an effect on the past and the present. In real life, the late Viktor Frankl, who was held in a concentration camp, often spoke about how people must have some sense of a future in life (Frankl, 1959). While he was imprisoned, he was able to use this idea to gain a sense of the future, which, in turn, influenced his present situation. These examples raise the question: What if the future could have an effect on, or even cause certain events in, the present or the past?

Consider these situations for a moment: If you knew that you were going to win a seven-digit lottery tomorrow, would you go to work? If you knew that something bad was going to happen to someone you care about, would you take action to prevent it? By knowing the future, your actions in the present can be influenced. Thus, I will discuss how cocreating preferred futures with adolescents and families can have an effect on the present and past.

Before moving on to ways of cocreating preferred futures, it is important to review some guidelines. Table 3.1 summarizes what therapists ought to consider when working to cocreate preferred futures with youth and families.

Let's examine a few ways that therapists can work with adolescents and families to cocreate preferred futures.

Crystal Balls and Beyond . . .

Milton Erickson had an interesting way of helping clients to envision a future with possibilities. By using the image of crystal balls, he would help his patients to create change in their lives (Erickson, 1954). After finding out what needed to change, Erickson would induce trance and have the patients hallucinate a series of crystal balls, with each one representing a situation and time in their lives. Then, he would have the patients peer into the crystal ball that

TABLE 3.1
CONSIDERATIONS FOR COCREATING PREFERRED FUTURES WITH YOUTH

❖ *Cocreate realistic and attainable futures.* Therapists must work with youth to establish preferred futures that are possible for the adolescents, given who they are and how their situation, resources, and capabilities affect their activities. Some things are unchangeable even though they may truly be what an adolescent wants (e.g., bringing back a deceased parent, having a driver's license at age 11 years, and so on).

❖ *Cocreate legal and ethical futures.* Therapists must make sure that preferred futures are within the law and ethical. For example, it is not OK to set a future vision of being a gang member if the gang is involved in illegal action. Some behaviors are OK and others are not. Therapists should support those future visions that are legal and ethical, and promote health and well-being; they must stand against those that are illegal, unethical, or harmful to self or others.

❖ *Pay attention to small changes.* Long-term or larger future visions may be established, but it is important for therapists to attend to whether signs or small changes indicate that a youth is still heading in the desired direction. There may be an overall preferred future that an adolescent or family member would like to attain, but attention to smaller goals or changes along the way can make a significant difference. When adolescents have the feeling that they are moving forward, they may feel less frustrated and more hopeful. It is also important that others (i.e., parents, juvenile officers, and so on) are clear as to what signs may represent movement toward established visions.

symbolized the future, suggesting that they could envision how they would be able to achieve the preferred outcome—when the problem would no longer be a problem. In addition, Erickson would inquire about what had been helpful in the psychotherapy: What had assisted in resolving the patients' concerns? Once he had obtained a detailed description of how the problem was resolved and the preferred future outcome, Erickson would suggest amnesia for the hallucination. The patients would then forget about the imagined future in which things had worked out.

After the patients finished the hypnotic experience, Erickson would suggest the actions described in the trance, as a way to resolve the problem and move toward a preferred future. Essentially, he helped his patients to develop, for the future, a blueprint of how they were going to resolve their problem. In Erickson's work with his patients, gaining a sense of the future seemed to have an effect on the present.

Although Erickson used trance with his crystal ball method, there are variations that can be done nonhypnotically. In my office, I substitute a dry-erase board, an assortment of crayons and markers, and paper for drawing. I have the youth draw a picture of three crystal balls or three "windows" that represent the past, present, and future. Next, I ask that they draw a picture of themselves inside each of the crystal balls or windows. Then, I ask several questions about the first two pictures, representing the past and present:

What are you doing in this (past/present) crystal ball/window?

What are you thinking about in this (past/present) crystal ball/window?

What are you feeling in this (past/present) crystal ball/window?

What would you like to have happen in this (past/present) crystal ball/window?

Next, I move to the drawing that represents the future and say:

As you look into this crystal ball/window, imagine that you are now in the future and things are going good for you. You're happy that things are better, and people around you seem to be happier too.

I then follow this with a few questions:

How did things get better?

Where did your problem go?

What did you do to help solve the problem?

What did others do to help solve the problem?

What other people know that the problem is gone?

How do they know?

What will you do if the problem starts to come back?

I often hear very interesting and ingenious stories from younger adolescents about how their problem was solved. Older adolescents may be less interested in displaying their artistic talents, so I will sometimes draw three circles on a dry-erase board and proceed from there. The idea is to get a glimpse of what their lives will be like when they are no longer being hindered by the problem. Once that becomes clear, steps can be taken to achieve that preferred outcome and future.

Miracles and Other Phenomena

Steve de Shazer (1988) and colleagues at the Brief Family Therapy Center (BFTC), in Milwaukee, Wisconsin, developed the "miracle question" as a way of helping clients to envision their lives when their problem is solved. The original form of the question is:

Suppose you were to go home tonight, and while you were asleep, a miracle happened and this problem was solved. How will you know the miracle happened? What will be different? (p. 5)

This is a useful question, particularly with adults; however, in many cases, I have found it to be a bit difficult for youth. Thus, I prefer a slightly different form. Here's what I typically say to adolescents:

Suppose that when you went home tonight and went to sleep, something strange happened to you and your life changed for the better. You may or may not know what actually happened, but you knew that your problem had gone away. What will be different?

Instead of using the term *miracle,* I substitute words such as *strange* or *weird.* Some people don't take well to the idea of miracles happening; others will readily respond. Words such as *strange* and *weird* can be broad for adults but seem to suit youth well. Interestingly, about half of the adolescents will come up with elaborate stories about what the strangeness or weirdness was and how their problem was solved.

Another idea is to substitute, in the place of *miracle, strange,* or *weird,* a word that a youth or family member has used during the course of therapy. There are many ways to use the original miracle question (or the question I have offered) to create the same image—how things will be different when the problem is no longer a problem. These types of questions can provide a glimpse of how youth might see their future when things are better.

For these questions to be effective, it is important to find out specifically what the youth will be *doing*—that is, what actions will be happening. The focus on actions moves the discussion into a realm in which the person has some choices and the power to make changes.

Videotape Descriptions

Several previous publications have highlighted the use of videotape descriptions in a variety of situations (Hudson & O'Hanlon, 1991; B. O'Hanlon & Bertolino, 1998; B. O'Hanlon & Wilk, 1987). I have found this idea to be particularly useful in helping adolescents to create futures with possibilities. Again, the idea is to have them describe a time down the road when things are going the way they like. In a recent publication, Bill O'Hanlon and I (1998) offered this example:

> *Let's say that a few weeks, months, or more time has elapsed and your problem has been resolved. If you and I were to watch a videotape of your life in the future, what would you be doing on that tape that would show that things were better? (p. 90)*

This method allows therapists to get action-oriented descriptions of how things will be when the problem is no longer present. It seems to be particularly useful with families because each person can describe what he or she will see happening. Parts of each of the visions of the future can be edited or spliced together, making a sort of "mission statement" for the family. One way to do this is to write each of the preferred futures on a little piece of paper and then ask the family members to put the pieces together in a way that works for them. They can use words, phrases, or whole sentences, but each person must agree on the final product. Then, the therapist can help the family unit move toward that preferred reality.

The Time Machine

Another way that is helpful in getting adolescents to catch a glimpse of their preferred future is to use a "time machine." Selekman (1997) has used this idea to help children propel into the past and the future. I typically use it as a future-based method. I want adolescents to get the sense that what they envision in the future can have an effect on what they are currently doing. Here's my typical pitch about the time machine:

Let's say there is a time machine sitting here in the office. This time machine can take you wherever you want to go. Now let's say that you climb in and it propels you into the future, to a time when things are going the way you want them to go.

I then proceed to ask the adolescent some of these questions:

Where are you?

Who is with you?

What is happening?

How is your life different?

What can you bring back with you to help you out in the present time?

How would it help you in the present time?

I can then work with the adolescent to apply the vision to the here and now. The following example demonstrates the usefulness of this technique:

Maurice, a 12-year-old, was in a gang and had been arrested for breaking and entering and for aggravated assault. He was asked to step into the time machine and head into the future. When asked where he had landed, Maurice replied, "In 2050. It's cool here. Nobody's hassling me. They're letting me do what I want."

The therapist inquired, "Where are you that nobody's hassling you?"

"I'm on earth," he replied, "but they don't care that I was in trouble before. Nobody knows now."

"How did that happen?" asked the therapist.

Maurice pondered this for a moment and then responded, "People just forgot because it was a long time ago."

The therapist asked how he could bring that back with him to the present, and Maurice explained that he could "be cool" for a while and not get into trouble, and then people would forget about what he had done. He described being cool in action terms by stating that he would not start fights any longer, not steal, and do his schoolwork.

FutureWorks

In the classic children's book *Harold and the Purple Crayon,* a little boy named Harold decides to go for a walk one evening (Johnson, 1955). All he takes with him is a purple crayon. But with his crayon he is able to construct a wonderful adventure. Just as Harold used a crayon, we can invite youth to construct artistic images of their preferred futures.

This is an extremely flexible idea. Adolescents can draw, paint, make a collage out of old magazines, make a board game, or create new ways of constructing their vision of a preferred future. Here's how I typically introduce this idea:

With the markers, paper, glue, magazines, and other stuff I have here, I'd like you to make something that will show me how you'd like the future to be for you (and your family).

As the "FutureWork" is being made, the therapist can ask questions or help out as the youth directs. When the work is completed, the youth can be asked about what is happening in the future and what could be done now to begin to move in that direction. On occasion, I'll ask whether I can add something to the FutureWork. If I receive permission, I'll put in an obstacle such as a magazine clipping of a liquor bottle, or I'll spell out a phrase such as "bad grades." Then I'll ask how the youth might deal with what I've added. At other times, I'll add something positive that I feel represents the youth.

Some adolescents ask to work on their projects at home. They bring them back (usually completed) to the next session, and we talk about them. FutureWork can also be a creative way to work with families. A family can create a collage, take turns constructing a drawing of their collective preferred future, or do something completely original.

Others have discussed the importance of attending to people's preferred views (Eron & Lund, 1996; James, 1890/1984; Rogers, 1961). With youth, this seems especially important because their stories about themselves seem to play an important role in overcoming obstacles, whereas others' stories about adolescents can be stifling. All of the approaches described here can help youth to rehabilitate or create their vision of a future with possibilities. We can then work backward, from the future to the present, to figure out what they can do currently, if indeed that is to become their future. When youth can envision and gain a sense of a future in which things are better, they create a catalyst for setting things in motion.

It's Not Always As It Seems: Mission Possible

Working with youth can sometimes make therapists feel that they are beating their own heads against a wall. Adolescents are masters at responding with "I don't know," "Maybe," "I guess," "Nothing," and an assortment of other colorful words and phrases. Here's an example of one such conversation between a therapist and a client:

THERAPIST: So, where would you like to see yourself down the road?

YOUTH: I don't know.

THERAPIST: What dreams do you have for yourself?

YOUTH: None.

THERAPIST: OK, what are your plans after you finish high school?

YOUTH: I don't have any.

THERAPIST: If you were to envision yourself down the road, say in six months, what would you see yourself doing?

YOUTH: Nothing. I don't think about stuff like that.

THERAPIST: What do you think about?

YOUTH: Nothing.

We've all had experiences similar to this one. The problem is that this conversation could go on endlessly, with the therapist eventually believing that the adolescent has no future, no possibilities. When youth seem almost nonresponsive, it is important to pay closer attention to anything that motivates them. For instance, for some youth, a preferred future is not having to come to therapy anymore, or getting their parents or juvenile officer off their back. Those *are* preferred futures! We can then discuss what their lives will look like when that event happens. What will they be doing, and how will things be different?

There will still be some trying cases:

A 17-year-old youth had been attending school regularly for all of his life. In fact, he had only missed two days during the current term. There were no reports of behavior problems with him, and he was a very nice, polite young man. However, he was repeating the ninth grade for the third time. When asked what he wanted to do in the future, he replied, "I don't think about the future. I'm just going to hang out now and see what happens."

Where I practice, adolescents with this view can be found in droves. Colleagues have told me of similar outbreaks where they live, too. These youth, although typically very friendly and pleasant, convey a sense of "going nowhere fast." Avoid the induction! These youth do have hopes and dreams—our job is to uncover them. Here's an excerpt of a conversation that took place with the 17-year-old quoted above:

THERAPIST: So you're not sure what you see yourself doing in the future?

YOUTH: No.

THERAPIST: OK, but I'm apparently missing something, because earlier you mentioned that you couldn't wait to get out of school. Is that your mission?

YOUTH: Mission?

THERAPIST: Yeah. You know, is it your intention to finish school?

YOUTH: I guess.

THERAPIST: How come? What will you be doing after you finish school?

YOUTH: Following the Grateful Dead around.

THERAPIST: So you're already a "Deadhead," but you'll be following them from concert to concert?

YOUTH: Yeah.

THERAPIST: That's interesting. I know they've got a huge following and there are lots of doctors and lawyers that do what you're talking about. How do people get into a position where they can live that lifestyle?

YOUTH: Well, a lot of them have jobs . . . some don't, but I will.

THERAPIST: So they work some, travel some . . . .

YOUTH: Yeah. And they work it out with their bosses.

THERAPIST: So you would need a flexible job?

YOUTH: Yeah. That's what I'm going to do. Find a job that I can make enough money and also take off when I need to.

THERAPIST: What will you need to do to find a job like you just described?

YOUTH: I have to either finish school or get my GED [general equivalency degree]. I need to quit screwing around with that.

THERAPIST: What would that take?

YOUTH: I need to talk to my school counselor and my mom.

Preferred futures come in many forms. As therapists, we can help youth to rehabilitate a sense of the future that has remained buried, or create a new one. In the next section, I offer some ways of questioning youth in regard to their preferred directions.

FUTURE PULL: MAY THE FORCE BE WITH YOU

Finding a Vision for the Future

The following list of questions can help youth in creating a better present and preferred future and can assist you in perceiving their visions and what they want for themselves and, perhaps, for others around them (B. O'Hanlon & Bertolino, 1998):

> *What do you think is important for you to accomplish during your youth/teenage years?*
>
> *What is your vision of a good future?*
>
> *What dreams did/do you have for yourself in upcoming days/weeks/months/years/life?*
>
> *What are you here on the planet for?*
>
> *What are teenagers/young people/human beings on the planet for, in your view?*
>
> *What area do you think you could make a contribution in?*
>
> *What would you try to do with your life if you knew that you could not fail?*

Dealing with and Dissolving Barriers to the Preferred Future

Some youth are clear on where they want to go with their lives, but they cannot get there because they perceive insurmountable barriers in their way. They fear success and they fear failure. They think they are inadequate to the task of making their dream happen, or they believe certain things must happen before they can begin to pursue their dreams. Here is a list of questions that might prove helpful in clarifying these perceived barriers (B. O'Hanlon & Bertolino, 1998):

> *What, in your view, stops you from getting to where you want to be with your life?*
>
> *What, in your view, stops you from realizing your dreams or getting to your goals?*

What do you believe must happen before you can realize your dreams/future?

What are the actions you haven't taken to make your dreams and visions come true?

What things stand in the way of realizing your dreams and visions?

What would your heroes, models, or people you admire do, if they were you, in order to make this dream or vision happen?

What are you not doing, feeling, or thinking that they would do, feel, or think in this situation?

What are you doing, feeling, or thinking that they wouldn't do, feel, or think?

Making an Action Plan to Reach the Preferred Future

Having a vision of the future, and even realizing what the perceived barriers are, will not necessarily take youth to that future. There must be a plan of action and a way to start to take some of the actions that can make the future happen. Here are some ideas and questions that can help adolescents and others to formulate and put into practice actions that will likely create their preferred futures:

What could you do in the near future that would be steps toward getting you to where you want to be?

What could you do in the near future that would be steps toward realizing your visions and dreams?

What would be a first step toward realizing your dream/future?

What would you do as soon as you leave here?

What would you do tonight?

What would you be thinking that would help you take those steps?

With most adolescents who are stuck in their troubles, just getting them to turn their gaze from the past or present to the future is a major reorientation. This reorientation can provide information about directions for treatment, introduce meaning and purpose into their lives, and lead to a restoration of hope.

PUTTING IT TOGETHER: THE VIEW-MASTER®

This case example may clarify how a change in the viewing of a situation can open up the possibilities for change in behavior:

A family of four came to therapy after the 14 year-old daughter began to run away from home. At the start of therapy, she had run away eleven times during three months. In describing the situation, the father said, "We don't know from one moment to the next what to expect. Her behavior is so erratic. Sometimes I just wish I could change the picture like you can with a View-Master."

The next excerpt occurred with this family during the initial therapy session:

FATHER: She's been unmanageable as long as I can remember.

MOTHER: For a very long time . . . it feels like forever.

THERAPIST: What has she done when she's been unmanageable?

MOTHER: She's always running away—mainly. It's weird because we don't know when she's going to do it.

THERAPIST: OK, and it seems as if it's been going on for a long time, and so far it's been hard to tell when she's going to run away.

FATHER: That's right. So how are we supposed to know what to do? Nothing has helped.

THERAPIST: Right. That's a dilemma for you. And one thing you'd like to figure out is what to do so that she doesn't run away. Is that right?

FATHER: Right, because we've tried everything.

THERAPIST: It's sounds like a frustrating situation and it seems to you like you've tried everything there is?

FATHER: Exactly. She just gets in one of her moods and it's like someone changed the channel or changed the picture on the View-Master; then she's really hard to manage.

THERAPIST: So let's say you had a View-Master and you could change the pictures at will. And, as you changed from picture to picture, they began to look more and more like the way you want things to be. What would be different in those pictures?

FATHER: She wouldn't be running away, and she'd be listening to us.

THERAPIST: OK, not running away and listening to both of you.

FATHER: Right.

THERAPIST: Anything else?

MOTHER: That's really it.

THERAPIST (TURNS TO THE DAUGHTER): Sara, how do you see things?

SARA: I'm not like that. I'm not always running away . . . or doing that stuff.

THERAPIST: OK, so you think they've got part of the story right?

SARA: Yeah.

THERAPIST: Which part?

SARA: Sometimes I run away, but sometimes I don't.

THERAPIST: That's a good point. What's that all about?

SARA: I don't know. Sometimes I want to go with my friends but not always.

THERAPIST: Sometimes you do and sometimes you don't . . . .

SARA: . . . and I've only run away one time in the last week. I'm trying.

THERAPIST: Really? How did you manage that?

SARA: I just didn't do it.

THERAPIST: So one out of the last seven days?

SARA: Eight days.

THERAPIST: So, on those seven days that you didn't take off, even though you may have had thoughts of doing it, what did you do?

SARA: I just decided that I shouldn't do it. It's stupid.

THERAPIST: How is it stupid?

SARA: My friend got hurt about two weeks ago. [Her friend was assaulted by another girl at a party.]

THERAPIST: I'm sorry to hear that. Is she OK?

SARA: Yeah.

THERAPIST: And you don't want that or something else to happen to you?

SARA: No.

THERAPIST: And seven out of the last eight days you've not run away. When you've kicked the habit, what will you be doing?

SARA: I won't be grounded, that's for sure!

THERAPIST (TO THE PARENTS): She's gone seven out of eight days without running away?

MOTHER: Right. She's done well recently.

THERAPIST: Is that part of what you're looking for with her?

MOTHER: It is. . . . She's capable of that kind of behavior, but we don't see it enough.

THERAPIST: So she seems to have shifted direction . . . and you want to see that continue?

MOTHER: Exactly.

THERAPIST: If she were to continue in this direction, would that signify to you that she's on the right track?

MOTHER: Yes.

THERAPIST (LOOKS TO THE FATHER): For you?

FATHER: Absolutely.

This session began with the parents' explaining that they did not know from moment to moment what their daughter was going to do. Further, they felt that they had tried everything to resolve the problem. Their story was one of impossibility—their daughter had been that way for a long time and probably wouldn't change. Nevertheless, it did not take long to create openings by subtly introducing possibilities through language. The parents were then able to shift their view from one of impossibility to one of possibility.

As I have described, these types of changes are possible with even the most challenging cases. The next chapter discusses ways of helping adolescents and their families to change troublesome patterns of action and interaction and contextual elements.

CHAPTER FOUR

One Thing Leads to Another (Except When It Doesn't)

EVOKING NEW POSSIBILITIES IN THE REALMS OF ACTION AND CONTEXT

Insanity is doing the same thing over and over again and expecting different results.

—Rita Mae Brown

AMY'S STATUS AS AN *eighth grader was legendary. Each morning, she would arrive at school on time, take her seat, and promptly begin to draw attention to herself by teasing and embarrassing classmates, talking loudly as the teacher spoke, or using an assortment of other tactics. After some time, the teacher would reach an intolerable level of frustration with Amy, feeling that the other students were being "cheated out of an education," and send her to the principal's office. After this had gone on for many weeks, the principal and teacher had a conversation about Amy.*

"She seems to really get under your skin," observed the principal. "What frustrates you the most?"

The teacher thought about this and then responded, "I can't seem to stop her. She just goes on and on, then the other students don't get to learn. We go through the same thing every day."

The principal asked, "What would you do if you couldn't get in through the front door of your house?"

"I'd use the back one," replied the teacher.

"That's right," followed the principal.

The next morning, the teacher went to her classroom and began as usual. When Amy began to disrupt the class, the teacher stopped and spoke to her. "It's clear that you are going to continue to do whatever you please until I send you to the principal's office. But you know, when you do what you do, it really gives me an excuse to not teach. I don't mind having a break. And I happen to like comedy, so why don't you put on your show so we can all watch you perform?"

Amy sat still, seemingly surprised by her teacher's reaction. The room fell deathly quiet. As she looked around the classroom at the other students, she noticed that they didn't seem to be the same audience that they were before. They somehow seemed different. Amy finally said, "I really don't feel like it today. I'm not really in the mood. Can we just do work?"

For the next two days, the teacher began class by asking, "Amy, are you in the mood to do your show today?" When she replied, "No," class would proceed. Amy finished the school year having visited the principal's office on only one more occasion, and that was to deliver some papers, having been selected as a principal's aide.

Just as the views that adolescents and others hold can be problematic, the actions they *do* can be troublesome. When problematic patterns are repeated, adolescents and family members may feel as if they're frozen in time or stuck in a time warp without a way of escaping. This chapter will introduce ways of helping to change and disrupt problematic patterns and interactions, and shift problematic aspects associated with context.

Before delving into how to change problematic patterns in these realms, let's do a short recap of the therapy process. First, we want to be clear about what the complaint is. To do this, we use action and videotalk. We then want to establish a goal that is both realistic and attainable. Finally, we want to know from the adolescent and family how they will know when things are better—that is, how will an adolescent, parent/guardian, family member, juvenile officer, teacher, or other person know that therapy has been successful or that change has occurred? What will the adolescent or others be doing when things are better? We also want to know what signs will indicate that things are moving toward the preferred outcome.

When we have an idea of what the complaint is and what change the adolescent or family is striving for, we can begin to elicit more detailed information about the problem. What we want to explore are *patterns*. Finding them involves obtaining action or videotalk descriptions of what the adolescent or others are doing that constitutes a problem. If a father claims that his son "acts out," we want to find out what the son has typically done when he has acted out previously. Even if a parent describes a problem that is internal ("He shuts down and doesn't talk and keeps his anger in"), an action-based description can still be elicited. For example, the therapist might ask, "If I was to watch your son shut down and keep his anger in, what would he be doing?" Or, "If you brought me a videotape of your son keeping his anger in, what would I see happening?"

Milton Erickson was fascinated with clients' problems and how they did them. He wanted to map out the details of his clients' problems. Erickson would focus on the problem at hand so intently that he might have been studying the person for a portrayal in a movie (B. O'Hanlon & Bertolino, 1998). Similarly, Neuro-Linguistic Programming (NLP) cocreator Richard Bandler, who along with John Grinder (1975; Grinder, DeLozier, & Bandler, 1977) meticulously studied Erickson's work, often has asked clients, "If I were you, how would I do your problem?" Essentially, both Erickson and Bandler have demonstrated the importance of learning people's personal patterns.

This position of curiosity is contagious. In a recent publication, Bill O'Hanlon and I (1998) described the role of the therapist in identifying problematic patterns:

> We explore with clients the negative problem patterns that seem to be inhibiting or intruding in their lives. We seek to be geographers, exploring the topography and coastline of Problem-Land. We want to know the details of the problem or symptom, *and* help the client to find ways of escaping it. (p. 66)

By isolating the problem, the therapist can intervene in the patterns that make up the problem, or change the contexts around it so they no longer contain the problem or symptom (B. O'Hanlon, 1982; B. O'Hanlon & Bertolino, 1998; B. O'Hanlon & Wilk, 1987; W. O'Hanlon, 1987; W. O'Hanlon & Weiner-Davis, 1989).

Adolescents', family members', and outside helpers' descriptions of problems help us to understand what they mean by the words they use, so our own interpretations are less imposed on their words. We're also searching for any aspect of a problem that repeats, indicating a pattern. The influence of Erickson and of the strategic/interactional therapists who followed has paved a road here. What we want to do is take a page from our predecessors and explore aspects of the problem pattern. To ferret out the patterns of the problem, we want to explore:

❖ How often does the problem typically happen (once an hour, once a day, once a week)?

❖ What is the typical timing (time of day/week/month/year) of the problem?

❖ What is the usual duration of the problem (how long does it typically last)?

❖ Where does the problem typically happen (spatial patterns)?

❖ What does the person, and others who are around, usually do when the problem is happening?

Here's an example of how a therapist might work with a parent and begin to explore aspects of a problematic pattern:

MOTHER: Joe just won't quit nagging me. He never takes "No" for an answer and bugs me until I finally give in. It's ridiculous.

THERAPIST: So Joe seems to nag you quite a bit and a lot of times he doesn't seem to accept it when you tell him "No." So if I was you and you were Joe and you wanted your way, how would you go about nagging me? What would you be doing?

MOTHER: I would pull at your clothes and follow you. I'd also block you from doing whatever you needed to do. He does that a lot.

THERAPIST: OK. And when would you typically nag me?

MOTHER: After school. Especially right before dinner because he wants to go out with his friends. Then maybe again after dinner.

THERAPIST: All right, and how long would you typically nag me?

MOTHER: As long as it took to get my way.

THERAPIST: Would you be nagging me in a certain room or place?

MOTHER: Usually I'd start in the kitchen, but it could happen anywhere and I'd just follow you wherever you went.

THERAPIST: Would I be by myself or would others be around?

MOTHER: Usually I would start in on you when you were by yourself. But even when Steven's [younger brother] around I'll do it.

Once a problematic pattern is identified, we can begin to help to change the doing of the problem.

CHANGING THE DOING

There are two ways that therapists can help to change problematic patterns of action and interaction:

1. Alter the repetitive patterns of action or interaction involved in the problem.

2. Identify and encourage the use of solution patterns of action and interaction.

Altering the Repetitive Patterns of Action and Interaction Involved in the Problem

The first way to change the doing of the problem is to interrupt or disrupt repetitive patterns involved in or surrounding the problem. Therapists' numerous options for doing this are outlined in Table 4.1 on page 94.

Continuing with the case involving Joe, here is how the therapist worked with the parent to interrupt the problematic pattern:

THERAPIST: I'd like to suggest something that might help you to resolve what happens between you and Joe.

MOTHER: I'm game because he's driving me crazy.

THERAPIST: All right. The next time that you tell him "No" and he begins to nag you, I'd like for you to walk into another room of the house, lay on the floor, and begin to hum one of your favorite songs [the mother was a concert violinist]. Could you do that?

MOTHER (LAUGHING): I could do that! He always leaves the room when I listen to "old people's music" (classical), so if I hummed it he'd probably leave.

THERAPIST: Great. Now when he stops nagging you, you can get up and discuss it with him further if you want. That's up to you. If he starts nagging again, then return to the room, lay down, and begin humming again.

The idea is to interrupt or disrupt the typical pattern of action or interaction. Often, only a slight change is necessary to cause a shift. Given below are examples for each of the variations listed in Table 4.1 for changing unhelpful, repetitive patterns.

TABLE 4.1
Steps for Altering Repetitive Patterns of
Action and Interaction

---

1. Change the *frequency/rate* of the problem or the pattern around the problem.

2. Change the *duration* of the problem or the pattern around the problem.

3. Change the *time* (hour/time of day/week/month/year) of the problem or the pattern around the problem.

4. Change the *intensity* of the problem or the pattern around the problem.

5. Change some other *invariant quality* of the problem or the pattern around the problem.

6. Change the *sequence* (order) of events involved in or around the problem.

7. *Interrupt* or otherwise prevent the occurrence of the problem.

8. *Add a new element* to the problem.

9. *Break up* any previously whole element of *the problem into smaller elements.*

10. Have the adolescent/other *perform the problem without the usual accompanying pattern* around it.

11. Have the adolescent/other *perform the pattern around the problem* at a time *when he or she is not having the problem.*

12. *Reverse the direction of striving* in the performance of the problem (paradox).

13. *Link the* occurrence of the *problem to* another pattern that is *a burdensome activity* (ordeal).

14. Change the *body behavior/performance* of the problem.

> 1. Change the *frequency/rate* of the problem or the pattern around the problem.

A woman came to therapy because she would become "overly upset" whenever her children disobeyed her. She would become anxious and speak rapidly and unclearly. It was first suggested that she find a time when she was alone and calm. She was then to speak slowly into a handheld audio tape recorder and say what she would typically say to the children when she was overly upset.

> 2. Change the *duration* of the problem or the pattern around the problem.

A 10-year-old who "threw screaming fits" that lasted five to ten minutes each time was told that he ought to consider screaming for at least twenty minutes to make sure that everyone who needed to know of his complaint was properly informed. It was suggested that his mother notify him if he stopped before twenty minutes. The mother only had to do this once. The boy exhausted himself in less than three minutes.

> 3. Change the *time* (hour/time of day/week/month/year) of the problem or the pattern around the problem.

Two adolescents, a 15-year-old boy and a 14-year-old girl, were accompanied to family therapy by their parents. The parents complained that the two adolescents were fighting (verbally battering each other) "like cats and dogs." The therapist suggested that the parents order the teenagers to argue spontaneously at a time when they were not fighting. Each of the adolescents was to be given five minutes to argue nonstop without any interruption from the other. At the end of that time, the other teenager would have five minutes. During the spontaneous argument, one of the parents was to watch the clock and the other was to make sure that there were no interruptions. At the end, the parents were to declare a winner. When the parents instructed the teenagers to argue, they seemed embarrassed and refused. The fighting ceased.

> 4. Change the *intensity* of the problem or the pattern around the problem.

An 11-year-old was frequently embarrassed by his classmates. His face would turn red during these times, which would increase his embarrassment. He was told that everyone has the ability to blush, but some are better at it than others, and he ought to practice blushing to see how many shades of red he could achieve. The boy later took pride in his newfound skill, pointing out to his classmates that they could not change their skin color on command like he could.

> 5. Change some other *invariant quality* of the problem or the pattern around the problem.

A 10-year-old would not go to school unless he had his favorite toy with him. A picture was taken of the toy and given to the boy to carry around with him. As children sometimes do, after a few days he forgot about the picture and became interested in other things at school.

> 6. Change the *sequence* (order) of events involved in or around the problem.

A 14-year-old would come home from school each day, throw her books down, and say, "I'm not going back!" The mother would then have problems getting her to go the next day. The therapist suggested that the mother meet the girl before she entered the home each day after school and say, "I can't believe the day you had!" The first day, the girl was so surprised by her mother's action that she only replied, "Mom, it wasn't that bad!"

> 7. *Interrupt* or otherwise prevent the occurrence of the problem.

A mother and stepfather brought their daughter to therapy because each evening, instead of doing her homework, she would argue and then not get it done. The therapist suggested that the next time the daughter argued, the parents should put her books away and go into another room and read or do something "constructive." During this time, they were not to talk with the daughter but remain "businesslike." The daughter was perplexed at her parents' behavior. After sitting alone for a while, she completed her homework.

8. *Add a new element* to the problem.

An 11-year-old boy would call his mother names and throw a "fit" whenever he did not get his way about something. The therapist suggested to the mother that she buy a small handheld audio tape recorder and turn it on each time her son started name calling and throwing a fit. The boy abandoned the behavior after his mother taped him one time.

9. *Break up* any previously whole element of *the problem into smaller elements.*

A husband and wife were having disagreements about how to discipline their son. Each time they would discuss a situation, the dialogue would turn into an argument. It was suggested that they get a timer, set it for two minutes, and allow each person two minutes to offer his or her point of view. Once the timer went off, it was the other person's turn. They were to argue one point at a time. When that was resolved, they could move on to the next concern.

10. Have the adolescent/other *perform the problem without the usual accompanying pattern* around it.

A mother brought her 10-year-old son to therapy because he would draw on the walls of his room when he became angry. The woman had tried numerous ways to change this behavior, all of which were unsuccessful. The therapist suggested that the woman make her son draw on the walls of his room when he wasn't angry. After doing this two times, the boy refused to draw on the walls any longer, and she was able to repaint them.

> 11. Have the adolescent/other *perform the pattern around the problem* at a time *when he or she is not having the problem.*

A man came to therapy because he would become irritated with his son, not talk with the son about it, continue to let the anger build up, and then, at some point, lash out verbally at him. It was suggested that over a one-week period when his son was at camp and he wasn't angry with him, the man should write down some critical things that he would typically say when irritated with his son.

> 12. *Reverse the direction of striving* in the performance of the problem (paradox).

A young boy was brought to therapy by his mother because he would throw temper tantrums on a daily basis. They would include screaming, crying, and extreme sarcasm on the part of the boy. It was suggested that the mother teach the boy the value of a good sense of humor by encouraging his sarcasm during each tantrum. She was to cheerlead and encourage him to improve upon his previous efforts. The boy became so frustrated that he refused to be more sarcastic.

> 13. *Link the* occurrence of the *problem to* another pattern that is *a burdensome activity* (ordeal).

A 14-year-old boy regularly came home after his curfew, was failing five out of six subjects at school, was frequently tardy to class, and would not do homework. Because he also was not studying, it was suggested to the parents that, on each evening that he came home late, they count the number of minutes that he had exceeded his curfew. Then, they were to go to his room and read to him for that amount of time, to make sure that he was getting his education. It was suggested that they do this even if they were both asleep and it was very late (they could hear him come in). The boy did not bring his books home, so the parents were told that they could read from encyclopedias or whatever books they had around. Any education would be helpful, considering he was missing out by not doing his homework and by being tardy to class. The parents only had to threaten to do this and the boy began coming in on time and improving in the other areas.

14. Change the *body behavior/performance* of the problem.

A 12-year-old girl would self-mutilate by using a tack, push-pin, or straight pin to carve messages in her arm when she was upset. She said that she would do this to see the blood. The girl was asked to use lipstick on her arm when she got angry, so she could still "see red."

Traditional strategic/interactional approaches that concentrate on changing problematic patterns by the methods outlined above typically rely on the use of *directives,* homework assignments, or tasks (Haley, 1987, 1990; Madanes, 1981, 1984). This approach directs the adolescent or family members to do what the therapist thinks will work. A possibility therapy approach is collaborative and does not view the therapist as an expert who knows the answers. Instead, the therapist and client system work to find some possibilities for changing unwanted or unhelpful patterns of action and interaction. Thus, the therapist only offers or suggests ideas that may be helpful to the adolescent and family. The therapist's position is one of curiosity or conjecture.

Another consideration when working with youth and families is the terminology used. The idea of "homework" can sometimes evoke bad memories for people. It can bring about recollections of meaningless, time-consuming assignments. If it becomes evident that an adolescent and/or the family members aren't or weren't the homework "types," it's probably a good idea to use a different frame. I prefer using the term *tasks,* but you may find another word that is better suited to a particular family or situation.

There are several ways that therapists can introduce ideas (tasks) for interrupting and disrupting problematic patterns from a position of curiosity. As discussed in the previous chapter, a therapist might offer an idea by using sentence stems such as "I wonder if . . . ," or "I had this thought . . . ," or "Perhaps . . ." Clients can either accept or reject ideas and suggestions.

To increase the likelihood that a task will be done, remain collaborative, and write down the task assignment and then follow it up. Families can post their copies on refrigerators, or wherever they wish, so as to have a guide to refer to between sessions. Writing down the task can also help to ensure that it is clear to the adolescent, family, or others. Follow-up is essential. It communicates that the task is something important that might help to change some unwanted behavior.

From a possibility therapy perspective, if an adolescent or family does not do a task, it is not automatically interpreted as resistance, but is understood only as communication—the family has communicated to the therapist that what has been suggested is not right for them. It is up to the therapist to explore with the adolescent and family other methods that might provide a better fit.

Ironically, tasks sometimes work best when they're not done. The mere act of constructing a task can change the problematic pattern. It won't matter that the task wasn't completed. The introduction of a new idea will have been enough to disrupt the problematic pattern. However, in the event that tasks are repeatedly not done and the problem persists, it can be helpful to discuss the fact that change often requires action. Bill O'Hanlon sometimes uses the following analogy to help clients get "jump started":

I keep firing the starting pistol and you haven't left the blocks yet. You say you want to reach the finish line (whatever the goal may be) but you're still at the starting position looking at me as if to say, "Why aren't I at the finish line yet?" What some people don't realize is that it will take some action on your part to bring about the changes you want. The task we discussed is the starting pistol. It is the way you get off the blocks and to the finish line. (Personal communication, 1997)

When family members make it clear that they don't have the time or don't see the task as a priority, the therapist ought to (a) do something different or (b) talk with the family about whether current circumstances (i.e., not enough time, lack of energy, and so on) are making therapy too difficult an endeavor, and whether they ought to return when they have more time or energy to focus on it.

A saying borrowed from the business world has taken hold lately: "Out of the box." An "in the box/out of the box" metaphor can also be helpful in psychotherapy. I regularly encourage families with youth to be very creative when they are trying to disrupt and change unwanted patterns of action or interaction. The following story illustrates how creativity can make a difference in changing unwanted behavior:

A retired man bought a new home near a junior high school. The first few weeks following his move brought peace and contentment. Then the new school year began. The afternoon of the first day of school, three boys came walking down the street, beating on every trash can they encountered. This continued each day until the man decided to take action.

One afternoon, the man walked out and met the young percussionists and said, "You kids are a lot of fun. I like to see you express your exuberance like that. Used to do the same thing when I was your age. I'll give you each a dollar if you promise to come around every day and do your thing." The boys were elated and agreed to continue their drumming. After a few days, the man approached the boys and, with a sad smile, said, "The recession's really putting a big dent in my income. From now on, I'll only be able to pay you fifty cents to beat the cans." Although the boys were displeased, they agreed to continue their banging.

A few days later, the retiree again approached the boys and said, "I haven't received my Social Security check yet, so I'm not going to be able to give you more than 25 cents. Will that be okay?" "A lousy quarter?" the drum leader exclaimed. "If you think we're going to waste our time, beating these cans for a quarter, you're nuts! No way, mister. We quit!" The man went on to enjoy peace once again. (Gentle Spaces News, 1995, pp. 297–298)

Creativity, spontaneity, and humor can inject a new element into situations where annoying patterns are repeated. Parents ought to be encouraged to stop doing what doesn't work and to think "outside of the box." A good way of helping parents to get their creative juices flowing is to tell them a story such as the one above or narrate what other parents have tried. The therapist can say, "I know of a parent who tried _____ . I'm not sure how it would work for you, but would that be something that you could try?" Or, after offering some examples, the therapist could ask, "What kinds of ideas do you think might be worth trying with the problem you're facing?"

Another way to encourage creativity is to suggest that parents try the "Do Something Different" task (de Shazer, 1985). This can be particularly helpful when the responses of parents have become predictable in the eyes of their son or daughter. Parents are told, "Between now and the next time we meet, I would like each of you to do something different, no matter how strange, weird, or off-the-wall what you do might seem" (p. 123). This prompting of parents to be spontaneous and creative is often enough to break up the monotony of unwanted patterns of interaction.

Identifying and Encouraging the Use of Solution Patterns of Action and Interaction

A second way of changing the doing of problems is to elicit, evoke, and highlight previous solution patterns, abilities, competencies, strengths, and resources (W. O'Hanlon, 1998). This does not mean trying to convince adolescents and others of their competencies and abilities. For example, we wouldn't say, "You can do it. Just look at your all your strengths!" This can be very invalidating to adolescents and families who are stuck. Instead, we might say, "How were you able to do that?" Or, "What is it about you that you were able to _____ ?"

We want to continue to acknowledge what is being experienced internally and begin to investigate, as would Sherlock Holmes or Columbo, adolescents' and others' wealth of experience and expertise. Through our questions, we work to evoke some sense of competence and whatever experience in solving problems they already possess. Sometimes, adolescents, family members, or outside helpers get caught up in problematic patterns and have difficulty recalling the experience they have within. I offer here five specific ways of encouraging the use of solution patterns of action and interaction.

1. *Find out about previous solutions to the problem, including partial solutions and partial successes.* Even when adolescents and families appear to be stuck, there are times when they haven't experienced the problem full force, or have expected to experience the problem but it did not happen. We want to inquire about exceptions to the problem pattern, including past solutions and partial solutions/successes. Here are some questions that may help therapists to find out about clients' previous solution attempts:

> *Tell me about a time when the problem happened and you were able to get somewhat of a handle on it. What was different about that time?*
>
> *You've run away on five out of the last seven nights. How did you keep yourself from taking off on the other two nights?*
>
> *You mentioned that you usually "lose your temper" and scream at him when he breaks curfew, but you didn't do that last night. What did you do differently?*

Once again, we are aiming for action descriptions of what people are doing or have done differently. We are also *presupposing* that there have been times when things were better (W. O'Hanlon & Weiner-Davis, 1989). We are not asking "if" there have been different or better times. We are asking what happened, when it happened, and how it happened to be different.

Let's take the example of the parent who typically screams at his son when he breaks curfew. Here's how a therapist might converse with the parent to evoke a solution pattern:

THERAPIST: On some previous occasions, you've lost your temper and screamed at your son when he's broken curfew, but you didn't last night. How did you do that?

PARENT: I just did.

THERAPIST: What is it that you did differently than the other times when you've been upset?

PARENT: I guess I just backed off.

THERAPIST: OK. You backed off in what way—physically, emotionally, verbally?

PARENT: Verbally. I didn't yell when I usually would have.

THERAPIST: Right, and that was different because usually you would have yelled. How did that come about, because you could have yelled?

PARENT: I just told myself it could wait until the morning.

Sometimes, clients will have a hard time relating what they did differently. In these instances, we can offer multiple-choice options. With the same example, we might say, "So did you find yourself being quieter than usual, or did you leave the room, or was it something else?" Multiple-choice inquiries will often lead to clarification on the part of the client. He or she will either affirm one of the choices or respond, "No, what I actually did was _____ ."

For many people, it will be too much to ask, "Tell me about a time when you didn't have the problem." Typical responses to such a request include, "I always have the problem," or "Things are always bad." Thus, as discussed previously in regard to scaling and percentage questions, it is usually better to inquire about small indicators of success or solution patterns. For example, a therapist might ask, "Tell me about a time when things went a little bit better." Smaller increments of difference will usually be easier for people to identify.

Should an adolescent, parent, or other person still respond that the problem is never any better, we want to do two things: (a) make sure we are acknowledging and validating what the person is experiencing internally, and (b) work backward from worst to best. Here's an example of how to do this:

THERAPIST: You mentioned that Timmy's behavior has been very bad lately, and that you're most worried about his tantrums. And when he has these tantrums he scratches and kicks you. Tell me about a time recently when he seemed to be a little more manageable.

MOTHER: You don't get it. His tantrums are always bad. Very bad. They just go on and on. He's relentless.

THERAPIST: OK. So it seems to you that his tantrums are always bad. So which day this week was the worst?

MOTHER: Oh, that's easy. It was Wednesday.

THERAPIST: What happened?

MOTHER: He was so bad he bruised my arm.

THERAPIST: Are you OK?

MOTHER: Oh yeah. It'll go away.

THERAPIST: Well, if Wednesday was the worst, what was Tuesday like because it wasn't quite as bad as Wednesday?

MOTHER: He did sleep a bit more on Tuesday. I guess he was more tired than usual.

The idea is to evoke and elicit small solutions patterns that run counter to the problematic pattern. Here's another possible way of working with the same parent:

THERAPIST: Am I right in guessing that sometimes his tantrums are worse than others?

MOTHER: Definitely.

THERAPIST: All right. What is happening when he's on the downswing and moving toward a calmer time?

MOTHER: Well, he just wears himself out, I guess.

THERAPIST: How does that usually come about?

MOTHER: If I just stand there and don't react, he will usually wear himself out quicker because he uses more energy trying to get me to react.

We want to acknowledge and validate adolescents' and others' experiences while simultaneously evoking their competencies, abilities, and previous solution attempts in relation to the problem. Generally speaking, it's helpful to use "solution talk" instead of "problem talk." For instance, a therapist using problem talk might ask, "Tell me about a time when the problem wasn't quite as bad." The solution talk version might be, "Tell me about a time when things were a bit more manageable for you." Solution talk can orient adolescents and others toward what's working, as opposed to drawing attention to what is not. However, as illustrated earlier, therapists will sometimes need to adjust if a particular client does not relate to such a focus. Therapists can elicit and evoke solution patterns just as well by talking about the problem.

2. *Find out what happens when the problem ends or starts to end.* The problems that families with adolescents have experienced have end points; they always come to an end, if only for a short while. Sometimes, solution patterns exist within these times. What we want to know is: How does the problem typically end? We can also ask for more details about aspects of the ending process. Here are some possible questions:

How do you know when the problem is coming to an end? What's the first thing that you notice?

How can others tell when the problem has subsided or started to subside?

What do you or others do that helps to bring the problem to an end?

What have you noticed helps you to wind down?

The following case example illustrates how a solution pattern can be found by inquiring about how a problem ends:

Aaron was verbally teasing and picking on his younger brother "relentlessly," according to his parents. They reported that they were frustrated because they felt their efforts to stop him were futile. The mother remarked, "I know older brothers sometimes tease younger ones but he's really mean and merciless." Aaron was asked, "You've got your parents telling you to knock it off, and you know it's not a cool thing to do, but how do you know when enough is enough and finally get a grip and stop teasing your brother?" Aaron replied, "When my mom tells me I'm gonna be grounded, I stop, but she doesn't usually do that until she's tried everything else."

By finding out how a problem ends or starts to end, we can also find out how a process might be altered or interrupted. Clients can learn choice points where they can intervene with solution patterns instead of continuing the problem pattern or allowing it to evolve.

3. *Find out about any helpful changes that happened before treatment began.* Pretreatment change can yield important information about how adolescents and families solve their problems. In an exploratory study at the Brief Family Therapy Center (BFTC) in Milwaukee (Weiner-Davis, de Shazer, & Gingerich, 1987), clients attending their first session were asked: "Many times, people notice in between the time they make the appointment for therapy and the first session that things already seem different. What have you noticed about your situation?" (p. 360). The study found that two-thirds experienced some form of positive pretreatment change. Two subsequent studies also found that over 60% reported improvement prior to the start of therapy (D. Lawson, 1994; McKeel, 1997; McKeel & Weiner-Davis, 1995). The following case example illustrates how pretreatment change can represent solutions patterns:

Phillip had been in trouble at school on a regular basis. With the school year in its final quarter, he had not gone for an entire week without having to be sent to the principal's office for disrupting the class. The school recommended that he see a therapist. Phillip was informed that he would be seeing a therapist a week later. During the week leading up to the appointment, he did not get into trouble at school. His mother called the therapist and said, "I'm not sure if I should bring him or not. I mean, Phillip hasn't been in any trouble all week and he hasn't done that all year."

For some people, just knowing that they have an appointment and will be beginning therapy leads to positive change. As with the case above, some parents of adolescents will say something like, "He knew he was coming so he's been on his best behavior." Bill O'Hanlon calls this the "flossing" effect; people will often begin to floss more just before they go to see their dentist. By inquiring about pretreatment change, we can learn how adolescents and families change, and we can elicit, evoke, and amplify what they've already done.

4. *Search for contexts in which the adolescent, family member, or other person feels competent and has good problem-solving or creative skills.* Even though adolescents and families may be experiencing problems in specific areas of their lives, they often have competencies, abilities, or solution patterns in other areas that can be helpful in solving the problem at hand. We want to explore any areas that adolescents, family members, or others feel good about— jobs, hobbies, sports, clubs, or areas of special knowledge or skill that can be tapped to solve the problem.

We also want to find out about exceptions to the problem. Sometimes, referring back to the initial interview can be helpful here. Information about school, social relationships, and contexts requiring competency and ability will have been highlighted. For instance, a therapist dealing with a youth who was having trouble completing homework assignments might inquire as to how the youth had been able to get the work done at school. Here's how one might explore various contexts with an adolescent who is struggling with fighting:

THERAPIST: So things haven't been going that great at home?

DOUG: If they'd just get off my case about the fights, everything would be fine.

THERAPIST: It seems to you like they're on your case a lot of the time because they're worried about you getting in fights at school.

DOUG: Well yeah, if people wouldn't say crap to me, I wouldn't be fighting.

THERAPIST: I can see how that might get to you. I'm curious, though; I haven't heard anyone say that you have been ejected from a football game for fighting or have even gotten a personal foul called on you. How have you managed that?

DOUG: That's different. I don't want to get kicked out of football.

THERAPIST: What do you do when there's a player on the opposing team starting stuff?

DOUG: I just ignore it and get down to business.

THERAPIST: How do you do that?

Doug: I stay focused on my job. My job's to help win the game.

Therapist: Would you be doing your job if you were suspended from school and had to miss a game?

Doug: No way.

Therapist: What do you consider your job at school?

Doug: Getting an education.

Therapist: How can what you do on the football field be helpful to you at school?

Doug: I guess I just need to realize what my goal is.

Therapist: What is your goal?

Doug: To finish school and keep playing sports.

When we can elicit and evoke abilities, strengths, resources, and solution areas in other parts of an adolescent's or other person's life, we can link them to the problematic area. In addition, we can find times when the problem doesn't occur or happens to a lesser degree. For example, I will frequently hear parents say things such as, "I don't get it; he treats us horribly at home but all I hear from his friends' parents is how sweet and wonderful he is." We want to explore these other areas and find out how they can be useful in solving the current problem.

We can also employ entire families to help solve problems. The following case example illustrates this point:

I was consulting with a colleague about a case where the family was "not getting along." The therapist, Kelly, described how the youngest girl was "disengaged" and depressed. Further exploration found that when the family played board games, the little girl perked up. The therapist was asked to find out what each person was doing while the board games were going on that was different from other times. Kelly discovered that the mother and father would sit together, the older sister would make popcorn, and the youngest girl would be in charge of some aspect of the game (i.e., being the banker). The family was asked if they could use their game-playing mode to help the young girl become more "engaged" and happier. The family did so by making sure the little girl was in charge of some aspect of daily routines.

5. *Find out why the problem isn't worse.* Sometimes it can be helpful to ask why the problem isn't worse. This can do at least two things. First, it can normalize things for adolescents and families when they realize that some people do experience worse situations. Second, it can yield information about what they've done to keep things from deteriorating. Questions commonly used here are sometimes referred to as coping sequence questions (Berg & Gallagher, 1991; Selekman, 1993, 1997). Here are some examples:

How come things aren't worse with your situation?

What have you done to keep things from getting worse?

What steps have you taken to prevent things from heading downhill any further?

What else has prevented things from getting worse?

How has that made a difference with your situation?

Brian's grades had been gradually declining over the past two years. During the current term, he was failing all but two of his classes in school. He was asked, "How come you haven't failed them all?" He responded, "They're too easy." The therapist asked, "Yeah, but you still could have not done anything at all and bottomed out. What did you do to keep things from getting worse?" To this the youth replied, "I just handed in my work." The therapist went on to explore Brian's method of not bottoming out, and was able to help him apply this method to his other classes.

When families with adolescents are asked why things aren't worse, they're often caught off guard. Such a focus orients clients to what they've done that has helped to keep the problem at bay. Sometimes, this can help to build some sense of hope when families feel that nothing is going right.

CHANGING THE CONTEXT

Contextual elements are those aspects of an adolescent's or family's world that surround the problem but aren't necessarily directly involved in the problem (B. O'Hanlon & Bertolino, 1998; S. O'Hanlon

& O'Hanlon, 1997). Aspects of context come in two varieties. The first involves time and spatial patterns. Time patterns tell when, how frequently, and how long the problem happens. Spatial patterns point to where the problem typically happens. Because time and spatial patterns were discussed earlier in the chapter, this section will focus on the second aspect of context, which involves cultural background, family and historical background, biochemical/genetic background, gender training, and any propensities associated with these aspects.

What we want to do is explore the patterns that come from these aspects and consider their influence in supporting the problem. It is important that therapists are careful not to imply that influencing factors are *causing* the problem. As discussed in regard to resiliency, adolescents and others are unique individuals and should be treated as such. Because an adolescent comes from a family that has a history of alcoholism, that does not mean that he or she will become an alcoholic. Or, having a genetic or biochemical propensity for depression does not necessarily make one depressed. As with the viewing and the doing of problems, we want to explore problematic aspects and patterns of contextual influence, and solution aspects of the context.

A 15-year-old male was referred for counseling because he was being violent toward his mother and classmates. He had an older and a younger brother who had experienced similar difficulties. When the problem was explored, the therapist found that the father had been a violent man, as had his father. The therapist asked a few questions such as, "How did you learn about how men should act in your family?" and "Where did you get the idea that violence was an appropriate way of dealing with things?" The therapist then explored solution patterns: "Who in your family has not bought into the idea that violence is the way to handle things?" "What are some other ways that the men in your family have dealt with problems?"

In every problem involving a contextual element, there are problematic influences as well as solution patterns and competencies. We want to search for the exceptions and solution patterns that run counter to the problematic patterns. A good way of exploring this domain with adolescents and families is to use a solution-oriented genogram (Kuehl, 1995)—that is, instead of doing a traditional genogram and searching for patterns of pathology and dysfunction, the therapist explores family lineage for exceptions and solutions. This alternative approach can uncover strengths and details that have gone unnoticed. Here are some possible questions that the therapist can use:

> *Five out of seven members of your immediate family led lives of violence. How did the other two manage to live violence-free lifestyles?*
>
> *Two of your uncles dropped out of school at an early age but went back to finish their education. How were they able to do that?*
>
> *You mentioned that all but one of your brothers and sisters have distant relationships with your father. How have you and your brother managed to maintain closeness with him?*
>
> *There are several members of your family on your mother's side who have died from alcohol abuse. But what I'm curious about is how your uncle was able to get sober at the age of forty-five.*

When solution patterns or competencies are identified, the therapist can then ask, "Do you think you have inherited any of those abilities?" This can give adolescents and family members the sense that things *can change,* as demonstrated by their family of origin. Solution-oriented genograms can also provide a different perspective in regard to contextual aspects, and can offer hope to families.

Context can also be used to normalize and highlight strengths. If an adolescent or family member begins to understand that, given the context in which the problem occurred, many people would experience, think, feel, or do something similar, it often lessens feelings of shame and isolation (S. O'Hanlon & O'Hanlon, 1997). For example, later in the therapy, the 15-year-old discussed earlier was complimented for standing opposed to the idea in his family that "men are tough and should do whatever it takes to get control." Aspects of context can be either problematic or helpful. We want to highlight those that promote problem resolution while simultaneously holding adolescents and family members accountable.

CHAPTER FIVE

Paving New Roads of Possibility

A COLLAGE OF CONSTRUCTIVE CONVERSATIONS

I vow to offer tribute to parents, teachers, friends, and numerous beings who give guidance and support along the path.

—Thich Nhat Hanh

A COLLEGE PROFESSOR HAD *his sociology class go into the Baltimore slums to get the case histories of 200 young boys. The students were asked to write an evaluation of each boy's future. In every one of the cases, the students wrote, "He hasn't got a chance." Twenty-five years later, another sociology professor came across the study and had his students follow up, to see what had happened to the boys. With the exception of twenty boys who had moved away or died, the students found that 176 of the remaining 180 had achieved more than ordinary success as lawyers, doctors, or businessmen. Astounded, the professor pursued the matter further. Because all the men were still in the area he was able to speak to each one. He asked, "How do you account for your success?" In each case the reply came with feeling: "There was a teacher." The professor found that the teacher was still alive and he sought her out. He asked her what the magic formula was that she had used to pull these boys out of the slums and into successful achievement. The teacher's eyes sparkled and she smiled. "It's really very simple," she said. "I loved those boys." (Butterworth, 1993, pp. 3–4)*

THERE ARE MANY PATHS TO THE SAME POINT

A possibility therapy approach does not rest on a set number of methods of problem resolution. There are many ways to reach goals. To this point, I have offered a variety of ways of helping adolescents, family members, and others to change the viewing, action, and contextual aspects associated with their problems. In addition to these ideas, several other types of constructive conversations can be very useful to therapists. This chapter will highlight a few of these as a way to introduce therapists to other possibilities. The opening story provides a lead into the first of these ideas.

115

UNCONDITIONAL CONVERSATIONS

People Who Make a Difference

What do movies like *Mr. Holland's Opus, The Karate Kid,* and *Dangerous Minds* have in common? They all portray the significance that family members, friends, teachers, coaches, scout leaders, and others can have in the lives of adolescents. Although the media highlight the profound changes that adolescents can experience by meeting well-known people, one does not need to be famous to have a positive impact on an adolescent.

If you ask people about their experiences of growing up, most will cite at least one person who, they felt, unconditionally accepted them for who they were and, perhaps, helped them through a tough time or two. Sometimes these people were family members or longtime close friends; at other times, they were only brief acquaintances. For adolescents who are experiencing trouble in their lives, a single person can make all the difference in the world.

Sean's family had moved to three different states in two years because of his father's relocation for work. During each of these moves, Sean experienced trouble "settling in." His mother described how he would enter a new school and "have enemies within five minutes." Sean was in fights with other students at school and in the neighborhood, argued with his teachers, had trouble with his grades, and frequently would not come in on time. He had been suspended eleven times in two years, and his parents felt hopeless about any change in the situation.

In an effort to curb Sean's behavior, the parents had elicited the help of multiple mental health providers, including psychiatrists, psychologists, and therapists. They had been through both traditional in-office counseling and intensive in-home therapy and case management. Even contacts with local law enforcement and the juvenile court seemed to make little difference.

When I began to see Sean, I explored many different avenues that I hoped might make a difference for him and his family. Despite our efforts, we seemed to take one step forward and two steps backward. Whenever things seemed to be going well, Sean would get into a fight or some sort of serious trouble. Then one day, things changed.

About five weeks after we had met, Sean and I were sitting on the front porch of his home when a truck pulled into the driveway across the street. This clearly sparked Sean's attention. A man stepped out, and Sean yelled, "Hey Mark, what's up?" The man turned, waved, and replied, "Not much. Come on by later." I asked Sean who the man was, and he responded, "He's cool. He helps me out sometimes. I just like hanging out at his house."

I found out that Mark was in his mid-thirties, was married, and had a young child. What was so compelling that Sean would want to hang out at this man's house? Even stranger, when I asked Sean's mother about Mark, she replied, "It's weird, but Sean really listens to him and respects him."

Over the next few weeks, with the family's consent, I was able to elicit Mark's help with Sean. What happened was astonishing. Not only did Sean's behavior change dramatically, but he seemed to take more pride in his schoolwork and began to help out with the care of his younger sister.

As therapists, we often don't recognize that there are significant others in the lives of adolescents who can make a difference. So how do we find out about these people? We invite adolescents, family members, and others into conversations about them. Here are some questions that can help therapists to explore significant relationships or acquaintances that youth might have.

For Adolescents

Whom have you met in your life who knew or knows exactly what you've been going through? How does that person know that about you? How has it been helpful to you to know that the person understood?

Whom do you look up to? How come?

Who has helped you through tough times? How so?

Whom do you feel you can count on?

When you're struggling, who knows just what to say/do to you to get you back on track?

Who has the right idea about you?

For Parents

> *Who in your teenager/child/adolescent's life seems to be able to get through to him or her? How does that person do that?*

> *Who (family member/teacher/coach/scout leader/other) seems to get through to, or is able to have an impact on, your son or daughter? How so?*

> *Do you know someone whom your son or daughter responds to and who would be willing to help out?*

If an adolescent or other family member has a hard time coming up with names of people, try saying something like, "When things were going better for you, who was around to help you out or make a difference in your life?" Then ask, "What did that person say/do?" Another possibility is to say, "Tell me about a time when you were feeling crummy and someone helped you out." Or, "Tell me about a time when things weren't going too well and someone helped you to get through it." Through these inquiries, the therapist can get an idea of what made a difference for the youth and can work to establish possibilities in other contexts that could lead to positive connections. For example, it might be suggested that an adolescent become involved in an activity that was previously enjoyed or could prove enjoyable (i.e., sports, clubs, hobbies, arts, support groups, and so on). In other contexts, by sheer interaction, the chances that someone or something might positively resonate with an adolescent are increased.

Self-Disclosure

We've all had the experience of being on a different "wavelength" from an adolescent, a family member, or another person. In instances when communication seems to be difficult, self-disclosure can sometimes provide the necessary connective tissue. Self-disclosure can also be helpful in other ways. Not only can it bring to light the "humanness" of the therapist, but it can also help to normalize the experiences of others. According to some reports, therapists' openness through self-disclosure is one of the most important factors in therapy (Bertolino, 1998b). In fact, it can contribute directly to change.

I was working with a 17-year-old, Gina, and her mother, regarding the daughter's "irresponsibility" with her life. The mother was most concerned about Gina's leaving the home at various times and not returning for several days. During these times, the mother would have no idea where she was, whom she was with, what she was doing, or, most importantly, if she was OK.

The therapy did not seem to be moving forward, so I told the mother and daughter about how I had been irresponsible as a teenager. When I was younger, I sometimes would leave and forget to tell my mom where I was going. Then, I would become bewildered when she got upset with me for not telling her or leaving her a note about what I was doing, where I was going, or, most importantly, when I would be home. I didn't get it. I just thought she was on my case about nothing. But I finally realized that what I was doing to her was very uncaring and disrespectful because she would stay up late each time worrying about me. She would do this because she cared about me; as a result, she would lose sleep and suffer in other ways. I certainly cared about my mom and wanted her to know that, so I changed my behavior.

I thought the story was fairly basic and straightforward, without any deep, hidden messages. At the next session, when the two women came in, the mother announced, "We're better now! Last week after we met with you we went home and we worked it out." Curiously, I asked, "What happened?" To this the mother responded, "When you told us about what you did when you were younger, we knew we weren't alone. You got through it and we knew we could too."

Therapist self-disclosure can also encourage adolescents and others to talk and can help to build trust. This is very important because youth will often distrust adults, making rapport difficult. As Lambert (1992) and Miller et al. (1995, 1997) have pointed out, the effects of the therapeutic relationship can account for as much as 30% of change in outcome. Thus, if self-disclosure can enhance the client–therapist relationship and contribute to change, therapists ought to be aware of its usefulness.

Another reason to introduce self-disclosure is that it keeps therapy collaborative. Adolescents and family members see the human side of the therapist instead of just working with a "talking head." Ultimately, therapist self-disclosure can lead to new pathways and possibilities that were previously unavailable through other means of conversation.

EXTERNALIZING CONVERSATIONS: REAUTHORING IDENTITY STORIES

Chapter 3 introduced ways of helping adolescents and others to change the problematic stories and attentional patterns that they hold. Based on their individual meaning-making systems and social interactions, adolescents, family members, and others create stories that are sometimes problematic. Stories are constructions of meaning and understanding, and they can vary greatly from one person to another (Berger & Luckmann, 1996).

In working with troubled adolescents, problematic stories can seem to take on life of their own; that is, an adolescent, in his or her own view or in the view of others, *becomes the problem.* For example, instead of being under the influence of troubling behavior, a youth becomes "trouble." Peers or others view the youth as characterologically flawed or "bad," therefore impairing the adolescent's *identity* story.

As previously discussed, stories are not set in stone; they are changeable. This is precisely what therapists aim for when problematic identity stories are detected. To change problematic or spoiled identity stories, therapists want to invite adolescents and others into conversations that lead to the reauthoring of alternative and less oppressive stories.

In addition to the methods previously introduced, a way of changing unhelpful stories and views is to use *externalizing* conversations (White & Epston, 1990). They help to separate the problem from the adolescent by determining the problem's influence over the youth. The youth is never considered the problem; the problem is the problem.

Bill O'Hanlon (1994; Rowan & O'Hanlon, in press) has offered the following eight steps as a guide for therapists who are using externalizing conversations.

1. *Find a name for the problem.* The therapist begins by working with the adolescent and others to collaboratively come up with

a name that fits the problem. Remember, the problem is considered separate from the adolescent.

Kyle had skipped forty-two days of school and had been referred for truancy. During the conversation, he and his family were asked, "What kind of a name do you think we ought to give this thing that's such a nuisance?" Kyle's father quickly responded, "That's easy. It's a situation of 'Mr. I. B. Truant' coming for a visit. That's what my mother used to call it."

Some names that are chosen will begin with Mr., Ms., and so on. This seems to work best with younger kids. More often, the names that are decided on are basic descriptions—"Violence," "Tantrums," "Aggression"—or common psychiatric labels—"ADHD" or "Conduct Disorder."

2. *Personify and begin to externalize the problem.* Once the problem has been given a name, the therapist talks with the adolescent, family, or others as if the problem is another person with an identity, will, tactics, and intentions that oppress, undermine, or dominate the youth, family, or others.

How long have The Fits been hanging out with you?

When Impulsivo Man whispers in your ears, do you always listen?

When did Mr. I. B. Truant first invite himself over for an extended visit?

3. *Find out how the problem has dominated, disrupted, or undermined the adolescent's or family's life or relationships.* The therapist explores how the adolescent has felt dominated or cornered by the problem and has done or experienced things he or she didn't like. The therapist can investigate several areas: (a) experiences or feelings arising from the influence of the problem; (b) tactics or messages the problem uses to convince adolescents of limitations or to discourage them; (c) actions or habits the problem invites or encourages the person or the family to do; (d) speculations about the intentions of the problem in regard to the adolescent or relationships; and (e) preferences or differences in points of view the adolescent has with the problem.

How has Mr. I. B. Truant come between you and your family?

When has ADHD recruited you into something that you later got in trouble for?

Why do you think Fighting wants to leave you without any friends?

It is important to notice that the language used is not deterministic. B. O'Hanlon (1994) stated, "The problem never *causes* or *makes* the family do anything, it only *influences, invites, tells, tries to convince, uses, tricks, tries to recruit,* . . . " (p. 26). The adolescent remains accountable for his or her actions.

4. *Find moments when things went better or were different in regard to the problem.* The therapist talks with the adolescent about moments of choice or success he or she has had in not being dominated or cornered by the problem to do or experience things the adolescent didn't like. This can spell "bad news" for the problem (Epston, 1997).

When have you been able to stand up to Mr. I. B. Truant?

When has the Temper Tantrum Monster whispered in your ear but you didn't listen?

Tell me about times when The Fits couldn't convince you to act out.

5. *Use these moments of choice or success as a gateway to alternate (hero/valued) stories of identity.* The therapist encourages the adolescent (and/or family members) to explain how the kind of person he or she is (they are) allowed having moments of choice or success.

What qualities do you think you possess that help you to stand up to Mr. I. B. Truant's plans for you?

What is it about you that you were able to go on strike against The Fits?

How do you explain that you are the kind of person who would lodge a protest against ADHD?

6. *Find evidence from the adolescent's past or present that supports the valued story.* The therapist searches, along with the adolescent

and family members, for people who have known the adolescent when he or she wasn't under the influence of the problem, and who can recall the adolescent's accomplishments, good qualities, or resourcefulness. In addition, what does the adolescent remember about his or her life that fits with the valued story rather than the problematic identity story?

> *What do you think your old gymnastics coach would say if she could hear you talk about standing up to The Fits?*
>
> *Think of someone who knew you a while back and who wouldn't be surprised to hear that you've been able to reject Violence's taunting.*
>
> *What can you tell me about yourself that would help me to understand how you've been able to take a stand against Mr. I. B. Truant?*

7. *Get the adolescent to speculate about a future that comes out of the valued story.* The therapist asks the adolescent, family members, or others to speculate as to what kinds of changes might occur as the youth continues on a path of resisting the problem.

> *As Marie continues to stand up to and laugh in the face of The Meanies, how do you think that will affect her family relationships?*
>
> *As you continue to get the upper hand with Truancy, what do you think will be different about your school life, compared to what Truancy had planned for you?*
>
> *How do you think your strategy with Hyperactivity will help you out in the long run?*

8. *Develop a social sense of the valued story.* The therapist helps the youth to find a real or imagined audience for the changes that have been discussed. The adolescent also can be enlisted as an expert consultant on solving or standing opposed to the problem.

> *What do you think Eric's stance against Misbehavior has shown you that you wouldn't have otherwise known about him?*

*Who needs to know that you've made a commitment to keep Mr.
I. B. Truant from hanging out without parental permission?*

*Who could benefit from knowing about your enlistment in the
Anti-Lying Club?*

The eight steps are merely a guide for therapists who want to
learn an alternative way of dialoguing with adolescents and families.
Once therapists are comfortable with externalizing problems, they
can modify this process or create a new one. Table 5.1 offers an
outline of how I typically use externalizing conversations with the
possibility therapy approach already outlined.

The following excerpts of a case involving an 11-year-old boy
illustrate the use of externalizing conversations, as outlined in
Table 5.1.

TABLE 5.1
STEPS FOR EXTERNALIZING CONVERSATIONS IN
POSSIBILITY THERAPY

1. Find out what the complaint is and what needs to change
   (use action/videotalk).

2. Give the problem a name.

3. Determine the problem's influence over the adolescent. This
   represents the *problematic story.*

4. Inquire as to what things will be like when the adolescent is
   no longer dominated by the problem. Also search for signs
   that the adolescent is moving toward that view (use
   action/videotalk).

5. Find out about times when the adolescent has been able to
   stand opposed to the problem.

6. Search for an alternative, *valued story* of identity. Find evidence that supports the valued identity story.

7. Develop a social sense of the valued story.

Ray was referred to therapy for being disruptive in class. The disruption included bothering other students so they could not complete their work, walking around the classroom when he was supposed to be seated, making animal noises, and talking back to the teacher. Both Ray's mother and his teacher at school were concerned and wanted to see his behavior change.

Ray was asked, "What do you think we should call this problem?" Initially, he seemed puzzled by the question. So he was asked, "Remember 'The Grinch Who Stole Christmas?'" Ray nodded that he did. "At first, the Grinch was pushed around by grumpiness. What's pushing you around?" I asked. Ray replied, "My mom says I got ants in my pants." It was agreed that Ants were the problem for Ray.

As the therapy proceeded, it was learned that Ants had been around the entire school year and were convincing Ray that he should get up, move around the classroom, and disrupt others. The Ants did this by convincing him that he wouldn't get in trouble. But Ray was upset; he felt the Ants were lying to him because he kept getting into trouble and missing recess.

Ray and his mother were asked what things would be like when he was no longer being pushed around by Ants. Ray said he'd get to go to recess, and his mother stated that she wouldn't be called at work any more to have to deal with his behavior. I then explored times when Ray had stood up to Ants' attempts to lure him toward trouble. Ray replied, "Sometimes I just sit there and don't want to play Ants' game." His mother identified several times when Ray had sat still and completed work or done tasks without becoming disruptive. When his teacher was contacted, she also provided examples that contradicted the problem story and revealed a valued one.

Over the next few weeks, instances of Ray's standing up to Ants were documented. These were shared with other family members and school personnel. During the last quarter of the school year, Ray was given a certificate for "debugging himself" from Ants.

Externalizing conversations can help adolescents, and persons around them, to reauthor stories that run counter to problematic ones. Valued stories can provide youth with a good sense of self and "being," which is crucial for young people. It should be noted, however, that some adolescents have difficulty with externalizing conversations. The method is not for everyone. It's up to the therapist to find a method that works and to converse with adolescents and families in a way that's right for them.

CONVERSATIONS FOR THE EVOCATION AND LEARNING OF SKILLS

Creating Stories and Metaphors

Throughout this book, I offer ways of conversing with adolescents and family members that emphasize the exploration of possibilities and exceptions. A primary assumption has been that adolescents often have the abilities, strengths, and resources within themselves, or in surrounding systems, to solve their problems. The therapist's job is to evoke and elicit those resources and to invite family members and outside helpers to contribute to the process by using their competencies.

We know that stories, fairy and folk tales, and metaphors can be valuable healing anecdotes in working with adolescents and children (Barker, 1985, 1996; Combs & Freedman, 1990; Gordon, 1978; Kopp, 1995; Mills & Crowley, 1986; Wallas, 1985). But what makes them so healing? First, they engage youth and hold their attention. Next, they allow adolescents to create new meanings and understandings that can lead to new possibilities. Stories and metaphors can help youth and families to move on by:

❖ Normalizing experiences.

❖ Acknowledging realities and natural experiences.

❖ Offering hope.

❖ Bypassing everyday conscious ways of processing information.

❖ Reminding adolescents and family members of previous solutions and resources (B. O'Hanlon & Bertolino, 1998).

There are no *correct,* single meanings that come from stories and metaphors. Instead, there are multiple meanings and understandings: each person can get something different from a single story or metaphor. Here's one way to think about this. As you have read the first five chapters of this book (from page 1 to this page), in what way have the stories resonated with you? Whatever new meanings or understandings you have created from those stories are right because they're yours. And, they're likely to be somewhat different from the meanings or understandings that your colleagues will ascertain from reading the same segment of the book.

Frequently, people ask me how I come up with stories and metaphors to fit situations that arise. Metaphorically speaking, it could be said that I "file" stories away within myself. Typically, an adolescent or someone else will say something that resonates with me and, through association, I'll recall a story or metaphor. For those who are just beginning to create their internal "file folders," I'd like to offer a way of constructing stories and metaphors that is relatively easy to learn and is very helpful when working with adolescents. One particular model, the Class of Problems/Class of Solutions Model, will assist us.

Class of Problems/Class of Solutions Model

Bill O'Hanlon studied Milton Erickson's use of hypnotism and found that the psychiatrist consistently used certain processes to help his patients solve their involuntary or automatic problems. Involuntary problems—for example, being anxious, becoming phobic—are not problems that someone can show you or produce on command. W. O'Hanlon (1987) referred to one of the processes that Erickson used as the Class of Problems/Class of Solutions Model.

To use this approach, W. O'Hanlon (1987) suggested that the therapist must first determine what the client's problem is and, from that knowledge, derive "an abstraction that is a *set* of the kinds of problems that this problem exemplifies" (p. 73). The abstraction represents the class of problems. Once this has been done, the therapist devises an abstraction that includes the kinds of abilities that people have to solve the problem. O'Hanlon remarked:

> From that set of abilities (the class of solutions), a specific intervention is derived. The intervention is a parallel communication and treatment agent for the specific presenting problem. The specific intervention is a metaphor of some kind (an anecdote or analogy), a

task assignment, an interaction, or one of the trance phenomena. These are designed to access or develop the ability that is needed to solve the problem. (p. 73)

For instance, if a child has a problem with bed-wetting, the class of problems might be described as lack of muscle control, and the class of solutions might be automatic muscle control. There are also other possibilities for the class of problems/class of solutions. In any case, O'Hanlon suggested that Erickson would focus on the class of solutions and work toward evoking the ability necessary to resolve the problem. The following case of Erickson's exemplifies this idea:

Erickson met with a 10-year-old boy who was having problems with bed-wetting. After learning about the problem, Erickson told the boy, "Let's just drop this talk about bed-wetting." He then proceeded to talk with the boy about a variety of topics, none of which included the bed-wetting. During their discussion, Erickson learned that the boy played baseball and shot a bow and arrow. Erickson then began to talk about how there are different kinds of muscles and how when you draw back on a bow string, and aim an arrow, your pupils close down and tighten up. Erickson talked with the boy about all the fine muscle movements and adjustments his body made every day in a variety of situations. (Haley, 1985, Vol. 3, pp. 127–130)

What Erickson did was talk with the youth about abilities he already had within—muscle control (class of solutions)—thereby using parallel communication as he was simultaneously talking about the boy's problem—lack of muscle control (class of problems).

This method is similar to the idea discussed in Chapter 4—search for contexts in which the adolescent has abilities or competencies. But there are two differences between these approaches. First, Erickson typically used the Class of Problems/Class of Solutions Model with involuntary actions. He would find out about the person and the problem, and would then *assume* that ability and competency existed somewhere in the person's experience. The method discussed in Chapter 4 involves overtly inquiring about areas of competence and ability.

A second distinction is that the Class of Problem/Class of Solutions Model is generally an *indirect* approach. Erickson would talk about abilities, and the person would unconsciously link the solution to the problem. The method discussed in Chapter 4 is fairly direct. The therapist talks about abilities in other areas and suggests that the youth can find a way to use them in the problem area.

Although conceptualized for involuntary actions and behaviors, the Class of Problems/Class of Solutions Model can also be useful in creating anecdotes for adolescents who are experiencing trouble with behaviors that are voluntary. Voluntary problems can be produced on command (e.g., skip school, fight with others), although a youth may insist that he or she does not have any influence in stopping or changing the unwanted behavior. (Remember, don't buy into stories of nonaccountability!) The frame for constructing stories, metaphors, and analogies is as follows:

1. A descriptive account of the problem is obtained (i.e., an action/videotalk description—how the adolescent does the problem).

2. An abstraction is derived, and it is placed within a class of problems.

3. A corresponding class-of-solutions abstraction is established.

4. An intervention is selected (i.e., stories, metaphor, analogies, and so on).

The following case example illustrates how this model works with adolescents:

Jenny was referred to therapy because she had run away on multiple occasions. The therapy did not seem to be helping; after six sessions, Jenny was continuing to take off. Sometimes she would be gone for up to a week at a time. Searching for a different way of approaching the problem, the therapist considered the idea that Jenny was just making poor decisions. He then wondered how he could evoke the decision-making skills that she already possessed. During the next session, the therapist talked with Jenny about how people make decisions every day. Each morning, they decide whether they're going to get up, take a shower, and get dressed; what they're going to wear; whether they're going to school or work, and so on. But what seemed to happen with most people was that, after a while, they didn't really have to think much about those things because they were more automatic decisions.

In Jenny's case, the class of problem was poor decision making and the class of solution was good decision making. The therapist made abstractions in both realms and then offered direct examples of decision making that people do every day without thinking about it. The Class of Problems/Class of Solutions Model can be used to construct anecdotes that can be offered to adolescents and families via direct or indirect means. Here's an example of using an indirect approach:

Twelve-year-old Scott was brought to therapy by his parents because of his violent outbursts both at home and at school. When he would become enraged, he would throw things, yell profanities, and threaten to hurt anyone who was around. In talking with him about his situation, I found out that Scott was an enormous basketball fan and played on his church team. In particular, he was a big fan of Michael Jordan. As we talked about basketball, I described how Michael Jordan is an extremely intense player who knows that he has to use that intensity in ways that are helpful to his team. For instance, Jordan, as does each player, has a certain number of personal fouls that he can commit in a game before fouling out. These fouls are not bad actions. They don't hurt anyone. But Jordan can't afford to commit technical fouls because those could really hurt his team by getting him ejected from a game.

Scott returned to therapy two weeks later and told me that he had not had any technical fouls during the week. Thinking that he was talking about one of his church basketball games, I replied, "That's great! Tell me about that." Scott enthusiastically remarked, "My teacher told me to be quiet and I didn't yell at her. Last time I did, and had to go see Mrs. Ryan [the principal]."

For Scott, the class of problems was poor self-control and the class of solutions was good self-control. These abstractions are loose generalizations. Another possibility would have been to use poor decision making as the class of problems and good decision making as the class of solutions. Then, I might have talked with Scott about how basketball players frequently find themselves in situations where they have to decide what to do. For example, if another player shoves them, do they shove back? I could have used a direct approach and assumed that there were times (which there were) when Scott had played basketball and had not lost his temper.

Erickson regularly told stories and offered anecdotes to clients as a means of helping them to change. Some people will have stories filed away in their minds; others find them in books, through movies and television, or from other people. Stories and other closely associated anecdotes are an excellent way of connecting with adolescents and other family members and of offering possibilities for solution.

KidsCan

Finnish psychiatrist Ben Furman has created an interesting way of helping families with young children move toward problem resolution. He has dubbed it "KidsCan" (personal communication, 1997). The idea is to help children to learn a skill that will lead to the solving of their problem. Here are the steps for using this approach:

1. Talk with family members without the child present. Get a description of the problem. Try to be precise about exactly what the youth is doing. Get a behavioral description (use action/videotalk). It's important to be clear about the problem so that a corresponding skill can be developed.

2. As when using externalizing conversations, give the problem a name. Humorous nicknames can be helpful; they somehow change the way people talk about their problems. According to Ben Furman, they also give the conversation more of a collaborative and creative feel (personal communication, 1997).

3. Determine the exact skill the child needs to learn in order to rid himself or herself of the problem. This can be difficult; the answer is not always obvious. The Class of Problems/Class of Solutions Model can be helpful here, although the skill needs to be as specific as the problem defined.

4. Give a nickname to the skill to be learned. The child can be brought in at this point.

5. Tell the child about the skill the adults want him or her to learn.

6. Develop a practice plan that will enable the adolescent to practice the skill that is to be learned.

7. Develop a reward plan. This should be a nonmaterial reward such as admiration, social recognition, a certificate, or a similar token.

Furman does not have the young child present until the skill to be learned is given a nickname because it is common for children to accept adults' telling them what to learn. Adults, on the other hand, do not typically like to be told what to learn and may disagree.

The following case example, contributed by Furman, shows how this approach can be used:

A young boy had the problem of not being able to refrain from hitting other children when they came close to him as he was moving from one place to another. This problem was named, "Nearness Allergy." It was determined that the skill this young boy needed to learn was to let other people come near him without being disturbed about it—the skill of not being disturbed by bystanders. The child was brought into the therapy, and the skill that he was to learn was named "People Slalom." To have the child learn "People Slalom," games were organized. One of these was to walk fast through a maze consisting of children, without touching any of them. The track was gradually made more difficult, and the boy was timed each time he went through.

As mentioned, Furman originally conceptualized this method for use with younger children. When kids get beyond ten or eleven years of age, they often become less interested in the playful nature of such activities, so I have modified the process for use with older youth. The main difference is to *collaborate with the youth from the beginning:* use the adolescent's expertise in identifying the problem, naming the problem and the subsequent skill, and designing the activity that will help to overcome the problem. Adolescents can use the therapist and other adults as consultants, approaching them as they would a coach.

In the following case, a modified version of KidsCan was used with a 13-year-old adolescent:

Cory was a bright, calm, sensitive young man who was doing very poorly academically. He got poor grades because he did not study well. Cory had trouble focusing on whatever he was studying and "soaking up the material." He had been put on two different psychotropic medications prior to beginning therapy, but neither had helped him. Once a description of the problem was obtained, Cory and his mother named the problem "Distractionitis." It was decided that the skill he needed to learn was to not be distracted and to focus long enough to learn what was necessary to do well on his tests. Cory came up with the name for the skill: "Getting in the Zone." During this time, it was learned that he had earned a black belt in both jujitsu and karate. In fact, Cory had experience in focusing very intensely to learn the necessary martial arts moves, but had not actively practiced in over a year. As a way of "reactivating" his focusing ability in order to "get into the zone," it was decided that Cory would practice his martial arts focusing techniques each day for 30 minutes before doing his homework. His practice paid off. After six weeks, Cory had improved his test scores in each of his classes by a minimum of 27%.

The KidsCan approach can be used in a couple of different ways. One, as suggested by Furman, is to put the youth into situations where they learn a skill based on the activities that they are doing. The idea here is that a *new* skill is learned. The second way, and the form that is consistent with the Ericksonian tradition, is to evoke an ability or competency (skill) through activities.

REFLECTING TEAMS

For years, family therapists used the one-way mirror as a format for teaching and developing strategic interventions. The basic notion was that family systems were essentially stable, with governing homeostatic mechanisms. However, in the late 1970s, the Milan group of Selvini, Boscolo, Cecchin, and Prata (1978, 1980) began to understand families as evolving and changing. In line with these observations and with therapies that were becoming more focused on meaning-making systems, Norwegian psychiatrist Tom Andersen began to introduce ways of using teams in a collaborative effort— reflecting teams.

Lynn Hoffman (1995) explained:

> This method asked a team to share comments on the conversation between the therapist and family while the family watched and listened. The family would then comment on the team's ideas in turn. This innovation proved to be a great leveler, modifying the concealment that the use of the one-way mirror had so long imposed. (p. xi)

When one talks about "constructive" therapies (Hoyt, 1994a, 1996a, 1998), such as solution-focused, solution-oriented, narrative, possibility, and collaborative language systems, the topic of reflecting teams frequently arises. Reflecting teams have helped clinicians to flatten the hierarchy between themselves and clients, to make therapy more collaborative, and to offer a continuum of ideas (multiple perspectives and realities). In working with adolescents and families, reflecting teams can be invaluable.

At my agency, we typically offer the use of a reflecting team by explaining that sometimes "two (or three, four, or five) heads are better than one when you're trying to get unstuck." We also explain the process thoroughly. More often than not, families are open to the prospect of getting "extra" help. There are literally dozens of ways of using reflecting teams, and new methods are being created as I'm writing this. I will offer a basic framework here.

The therapist begins by meeting with the adolescent, parent(s), or family for thirty to thirty-five minutes. During this time, behind a one-way mirror, in a room with a video and audio monitor, or in the same room as the clients, a group of two to five people observes the conversation and interaction. I have found it better to limit the team to five members so that each person can share his or her ideas in a timely manner. This also helps to guard against the adolescent's or family's becoming overwhelmed or intimidated by having too many people present.

As the session begins, the therapist asks a few questions. Generally recognized as the developer of reflecting teams, psychiatrist

Tom Andersen (1991) has suggested two overarching questions that I have found useful in working with adolescents. The first has to do with the history of having a reflecting team: "Who had the idea?" This is followed with: "How did various others respond to the idea?" And: "Were all in favor, or were some reserved?" (p. 21). These questions help to determine who is most interested in speaking and who is less interested. The second overarching question is: "Who would like to talk about how we can best use this meeting?" This helps to determine what needs to be discussed.

Once the therapist is clear on how the adolescent, family, or other person wants to use the time, the session continues in the same tradition as other sessions. After time has elapsed, the therapist and adolescent/parent/family switch places with the reflecting team members. The members of the reflecting team then discuss their observations with each other as the therapist and adolescent/parent/family observe them.

The discussion among the team members remains solely among themselves; there is no interaction with the adolescent or family. Comments are made from a position of conjecture and curiosity, and emphasis is on competencies. The team members offer observations, speculate, and ask questions that are from a position that engenders hope. Here is an example of how three members of a reflecting team conversed about a family of five that had been dealing with multiple school problems:

THERAPIST 1: I was struck by how Mrs. Lawson was willing to do whatever it takes to get her family back on track.

THERAPIST 2: Me too. It's clear that they've been through a lot both as individuals and as a family. I have to wonder: What's the glue that's kept them together?

THERAPIST 3: I was wondering that too. At the same time, I was curious about how Chris was able to get himself back on track with school after missing twenty days. He knew it was going to be tough to answer all the questions his classmates were going to ask and that there might be rumors. That's impressive.

THERAPIST 2: It sure is. Maybe it's because he's more mature now or maybe he just realized that he didn't want to lead his life the way he was.

Therapist 1: I'm also curious to see what plans Josh will be considering for getting the upper hand with his grades.

One of the operational—and hopeful—assumptions here is that, as the members of the reflecting team talk, something will be said that resonates with each person present. Or, something said will make a difference for one person and will lead to a domino or ripple effect in the realm of change. At the very least, something that is said may lead to the construction of meaning for one person, who will take action. Sometimes, this action person is the therapist, who has gained a new perspective on how to help the adolescent or family.

If the reflecting team is observing for the benefit of more than one person, I suggest that something be said about each person who is present. However briefly, each person should be positioned at "center stage" for a moment. Just a little personal attention can make a big difference in what people experience.

After the members of the team have talked with each other for five to ten minutes, the two groups switch back. The therapist then spends the closing moments of therapy asking about what was experienced. A good question to begin with can be: "What was your experience like with the reflecting team?" Other possible questions include: "What did you hear/see/observe/feel?" "What was helpful about the process?" "What made sense to you?" "What new ideas do you have?"

Reflecting teams have been and can be used at any point during therapy. Over the past decade, many innovative versions of this approach have appeared, as ways of helping individuals, couples, and families to become unstuck (Friedman, 1995). More importantly, from the perspective of clients, research has found reflecting teams to be very helpful (Evans et al., 1994; Katz, 1991; Sells, Smith, Coe, Yoshioka, & Robbins, 1994; T. Smith, Yoshioka, & Winton, 1993). Among the derivatives of reflecting teams are conversational teams (Bertolino, 1998), which are similar to reflecting teams in the use of language but have a major difference: the therapist, client(s), and team members speak directly to one another. In any variation, these formats can be very useful in helping families and adolescents to get unstuck.

CHAPTER SIX

The World Where You Live

REWRITING YOUTH STORIES IN FUTURE SESSIONS AND BEYOND

I've got this preoccupation with ordinary people pursued by larger forces.

—Steven Spielberg

Life is out to get you.

—Steve Gilligan

A FEW YEARS AGO *an extremely upset mother called me. She told me a very sad story that moved me to tears. She spoke about how her 12-year-old son, Kyle, had been beaten severely by three teenagers. He had been hurt so badly that he nearly died. Now, some nine months after the incident, Kyle's physical injuries had healed, but his emotional scars remained. She went on to describe how her son would hide when he heard thunder, cry hysterically when she raised her voice at him, and was scared that the boys who had assaulted him would return and hurt him again. She stated that all of this was now affecting his social relationships and school situation.*

I had a full caseload with a waiting list of six weeks and was in no position to take another case. Even though I wanted to help, I realized that I was going to have to refer the woman to someone or someplace else. Just as I was about to do so, she tearfully said, "I've tried to get help but I don't have insurance. Each person I talk with just gives me another number to call. I'm so worried about him." All I could say to her was, "Can you come in on Monday?"

I saw Kyle and his mother on a stormy Monday evening. The boy was friendly, but understandably apprehensive and quiet. He seemed to be very withdrawn. The session lasted about an hour and a half, and I didn't think much about it after they left. I just planned on seeing both of them at the next appointment, which, due to scheduling restrictions, was set up for two weeks later.

Three days after the first session, the mother called and said, "It was storming badly when we left, but Kyle didn't react to the thunder and lightning. At first I thought it was because he was absorbed in thought or just keeping to himself, but then the same thing happened today. He was outside playing wiffle ball and it started to thunder, but he didn't flinch. He just kept playing—laughing and playing. I couldn't believe it."

Due to a death in the family, the mother canceled the next scheduled appointment. When we were able to meet again, I saw a boy who was talkative, humorous, and excited about his new roller hockey team. Kyle spoke about what he was going to be doing and what his

*plans were. His mother radiated with joy. The therapy ended after
that second session.*

*Recently, I received the following voice mail message at my office,
"It's been three years now and I wanted you to know that Kyle still
talks about the 'healing talk' you two had. I'm so happy that he's feeling good about himself and doing well. I just wanted to thank you."*

Milton Erickson believed that people could change rapidly. He did
not hold the adage, "If a problem took a long time to develop, then
it will take a long time to go away." In fact, he had many one-session
"cures" (W. O'Hanlon & Hexum, 1990). Erickson stated:

> Illness can come on all of a sudden; one can make a massive re-
> sponse all at once to a particular thing. I do not think we need to
> presuppose or propound some long, drawn-out causation and a
> long, drawn-out therapeutic process. You see, if illness can occur
> suddenly, then therapy can occur quite as suddenly. (Erickson,
> 1983, p. 71)

Change that *lasts* can happen very quickly. Thus, I am not surprised when I hear of an adolescent changing his or her actions, resolving a trauma, or overcoming an obstacle rapidly. In fact, I expect
change, and I work as a "changologist" when I see youth and families. Along with family members, I search for evidence of change
occurring in the direction of the desired goals.

Sometimes, in-between-session changes are so significant that
therapy is terminated after just one meeting. In addition, as discussed in Chapter 1, clients often get what they came for in just
one session (Talmon, 1990). Thus, our focus is on making the most
of each session by gaining clarity on what needs to change, and by
finding out how adolescents and families will know when things
are better. This chapter discusses ways of continuing this process
in second and subsequent sessions.

ARE WE THERE YET? FUTURE SESSIONS AND BEYOND

As with first sessions, when adolescents and families return for second and subsequent therapy appointments, we want to allow each
person to have the space to begin where he or she wants to begin.

Again, this does not mean that people have to ramble on aimlessly in order to feel heard and understood. As they speak, we want to use a combination of acknowledgment and possibility-laced language while simultaneously gathering information about what has happened in between sessions.

We begin second and subsequent sessions by asking fairly neutral questions: "Where would you like to begin?" or "How have things been since we last met?" Another possibility is to summarize where things left off in the last session, and then ask the adolescent or family members about what has transpired since. Here's how I typically do this:

The Wilson family came for their second session one week after their first. After greeting everyone, I offered the following brief summary followed by a question: "Last week you mentioned that things had been very tense around the house. Part of this was because Carla had been home just three days from her latest run. You mentioned that that was your biggest concern. You were worried that she might take off again and it was like being on pins and needles, waiting to see what would happen. Your sense was that maybe she was beginning to see things differently because, over the three days that she was home, she was talking to you more openly than before; but because it had only been a few days, you were still apprehensive. So, how have things been since then?"

By summarizing what happened in the previous session and finishing with a question, the therapist can begin to find out whether things are better, so-so, or the same/worse. Sometimes, this will become evident in the first few moments of the session; at other times, the status is not so clear. If it is not apparent, the therapist can ask a number of questions:

Can you tell me a little bit about how things are in relation to last time?

What's your sense about how things are going now, as compared to last time?

Last time, on a scale of one to ten, you mentioned that things were a five. Where would you say things are right now?

It is important to translate vague words into clear descriptions or action language. For instance, if a parent says, "Well, things are better," the therapist will want to inquire, "What specifically did you notice happening that showed you that things were improved?" Or, "What's going on that is an improvement over last time?" Once the adolescent or family members have conveyed a sense of whether things are better, so-so, or same/worse, the therapist can proceed in any number of ways.

Between-Session Tasks

A consideration during second and subsequent sessions is tasks. If one was offered during the first session, the therapist will want to follow up on whether it was done. One popular task that is frequently used is the *first session formula task* (de Shazer, 1985). At the end of the first session, the individual, family, or couple is told:

Between now and the next time we meet, we [I] would like you to ob-serve, so that you can describe to us [me] next time, what happens in your [pick one: family, life, marriage, relationship] that you want to continue to have happen. (p. 137)

At the start of the second session, the therapist asks the family members what they observed that they would like to have continue. This can be a very useful question with families. It helps to orient them toward what is working in their lives. It can also provide a step-ping stone into other areas of competency and change.

A word of caution: some families with adolescents will not want to delve right into this type of question. They will have agendas and will want to be heard, acknowledged, and understood before look-ing at what they're satisfied with in their lives. Here's one way to think about this: When you come home from work or school, does someone ask you, "What happened during your day that you want to have continue to happen?" Probably not. And if someone did, how would you react? Thus, if an adolescent or family member does not respond favorably to the first-session task, or other tasks, the ther-apist must be respectful of that and shift gears.

BETTER, SO-SO, OR SAME OR WORSE?

When Things Are Better

When the reports rendered indicate that things have improved, we want to find out in what way things are better, to what extent they have improved, and how the improvement happened. To do this, we ask questions that help to amplify the changes and associated solution patterns. Here are some examples of questions to ask:

What have you noticed that's changed with your situation?

What specifically seems to be going better?

Who first noticed the change?

When did you first notice that things had changed?

How did the change come about?

How did you get yourself to do that?

What did you do differently?

What did you tell yourself?

Who else noticed the change?

By using questions like these, changes that have occurred in relation to the problem can be more easily identified. The questions also serve as a way of amplifying any identified change. Furthermore, using exception-oriented questions can be especially helpful in drawing out solution patterns and actions that have contributed to change. Families can then be clearer about what seems to work for them.

Many times, when change has occurred with an adolescent or a family, there's more than meets the eye; other ripples or small movements may be present but are not so clear. As changologists, we want to continue to explore: "What else?" To find out about other changes, we can ask: "What else have you noticed that's different?" Or, "What else has changed?" Again, we amplify any additional changes that are identified.

When change has been identified and amplified, the therapist will want to get an idea of how that change is situated in relation to the problem. Does the adolescent (or the family, or others) feel that the change indicates that the problem has been resolved? Have the initial treatment goals been met? We want to know how the change relates to the overall goals of therapy. To find this out, we can ask an assortment of questions:

> *Last time, you indicated that if your daughter was able to get back on track with her school attendance, you would know that things were better. Now that she's gone for two weeks straight, how do you see things?*

> *You mentioned last time that if your son was able to make it to class, on time, nineteen out of twenty days, that would represent an eight. Now that he's done that, what else, if anything, do you feel needs to happen?*

> *How does the change that's happened relate to the goals we set in the first/last session?*

> *What else, if anything, needs to happen so that you'll be convinced that the problem is no longer a problem?*

USE SPECULATION

On several occasions, I have referred to the use of *conjecture*. It allows the therapist to speak about things—in this case, change—without drawing conclusions or trying to establish truths. When change has happened, it can be helpful to speculate, from a position of curiosity, what may have contributed to the change.

Speculation in this sense means offering possible interpretations as to what has contributed to the change. For instance, when change is identified, it is usually followed up with questions such as "What did you do differently?" and "How did you do that?" If clients respond with, "I don't know" or something similar, a possibility is to speculate as to how the change came about. When I do this, I usually speculate about things that are unlikely to be rejected by a youth or a parent. These include, but are not limited to, age, maturity, becoming wiser, and thinking more of other people's feelings. Here is how to do this:

DIANE (MOTHER): She has done well since the last time we saw you. I really haven't had to get on her about getting up on time and making it to school on time.

THERAPIST (TO DAUGHTER CARRIE): That's great! How have you done that?

CARRIE: I just did it. I don't know.

THERAPIST: That's OK if you're not sure. It may become clearer as you go along. But I have to wonder if part of it is because you're getting older and more mature and are making better decisions, or if it's related to your thinking more about your future and how your education might open up doors for you. Other people might say that you're just thinking more of others. Who knows?

Again, the idea is to offer some possibilities as to how the change came about that are not likely to be rejected by the youth or others. Most adolescents will not say, "No, I'm not getting more mature!" When I do this, it's common to see the adolescent and the family members perk up and smile. It's also helpful to use this type of speculation as an adjunct when people can identify what is different. For example, if a youth says, "I knew I better stop so I focused on something else," I might add, "That's great that you were able to focus on something else. I wonder if that's in any way related to your growing up and getting wiser."

It is not necessary that youth respond to speculation. If they do, the therapist can follow along. If not, just the mere mention of something that may have contributed to the change ensures that a youth or others will think about it and consider it at least momentarily as a possibility. We are merely highlighting those aspects that may facilitate change and promote an improved sense of self while simultaneously holding youth accountable for all their actions, good or bad.

MOVE TO AN EXPERIENTIAL LEVEL

Change is not solely an internal or an external phenomenon. It involves a combination of both realms. For some persons, an invitation to experience change at an internal, experiential level can be significant (Bertolino, 1998b). Similarly, when *some* families with adolescents are able to connect with an experience internally, it is more profound. Thus, with youth, it can be helpful to move to an experiential level when change is evident. The therapist can ask, "What

was that like for you, that _____ happened?" Or, "When you
saw your son/daughter do _____ , how did you feel?"

KEEP THE BALL ROLLING

When it is clear where things are in relation to the established goals,
it can be helpful for the therapist to explore with the adolescent and
family what will help to keep things going in the desired direction.
The therapist can ask, "What will you be doing to keep things going
in the right direction?" Or, "How will you be keeping things moving
forward?" "What else?" can be the follow-up question.

ANTICIPATE ROADBLOCKS, HURDLES, AND PERCEIVED BARRIERS

Another area to explore with adolescents and families is possible
roadblocks, hurdles, or barriers that might come up in between sessions or after the therapy has ended. This area is especially important because we want to increase the likelihood that changes will
continue (W. O'Hanlon & Weiner-Davis, 1989). I sometimes ask,
"Can you think of anything that might come up over the next few
weeks/month, or until we meet again, that *might* present a challenge
for you in staying on track?" Or, "Is there anything that might happen in the near future that might pose a threat to all the changes
you've made?" If the person answers "Yes," we want to explore, in
detail, what that challenge might be, and then inquire, "How will
you handle it differently than before?"

The following case excerpt illustrates how a therapist might discuss this with a family:

THERAPIST: So you feel like things are headed in the right direction?

FATHER: Yeah. I mean he's really made some strides with his temper.

THERAPIST: Good. Now, can you think of anything that might come
up that might be a challenge to keeping things going well?

FATHER: The only thing I can think of might be when he goes to his
mother's next weekend. Sometimes he doesn't get along too well
with his stepfather.

SON: That's just once in a while.

THERAPIST: OK, so it's a once-in-a-while thing. What's something which might come up at your mom's that could pose a challenge to you staying on track?

SON: I guess if he got in my face.

THERAPIST: Being where you are now, how would you handle it differently this time?

SON: I'd just tell my mom I'm not staying if he does that to me. She would step in. Or, if it was too bad, I'd just call my dad and tell him to come and get me. But I think it will be OK.

Family members are in charge of determining when enough gain has been made to schedule the appointments less frequently, or to end therapy. If it is not clear what to do and no one has voiced an opinion, the therapist can ask, "How do you think we should proceed at this point? Would you like to meet again or . . . " If the family wishes to schedule another appointment, the therapist can say, "When would you like to come back?" I sometimes find that parents will defer to me and ask, "What do people usually do?" To this I usually respond (unless I have a strong opinion), "It really does vary. My sense is that we should go with what you're most comfortable with. If, in the future, we need to meet more—or less—often, we can adjust."

Sometimes, spreading out the time in between sessions can be helpful as a way to measure change over time. I frequently do this when I have a limited number of sessions. For example, I might meet with an adolescent and his or her mother for two consecutive weeks and then schedule the next session for two weeks after that. I've even seen families once a month or every six to eight weeks. I sometimes refer to these sessions as "checkups." In any case, the therapist should collaborate with the family and come to an agreement with which they feel most comfortable.

When Things Are So-So

Family members will sometimes be ambivalent about change. They will say, "Well, he did a little better, but he's still doing other things." Or, "It's really hard to tell how things are going." There are two considerations here. First, we can help to normalize the experiences of family members by saying to them, "Sometimes, change is three steps forward and two steps back." This can put change into perspective and help to shift "all-or-nothing" views.

A second consideration is that we want to remember to continue to acknowledge and validate what adolescents and parents experience. If this is not done, some will have difficulty shifting their attention to the realm of change and possibility. We can then begin to subtly explore any traces of change. Here's an example of how to do this:

THERAPIST: So how have things been over the past two weeks?

MOTHER: It's hard to tell. I mean, he hasn't run away, but he still doesn't listen to us. It's frustrating.

THERAPIST: I can see how it might be frustrating to you because some things are looking up while others don't seem to be going in the direction you'd like. What I'm curious about is, even though some things seem to be the same, the problem of running away improved. How did that happen?

MOTHER: It is surprising. I wish I knew what happened.

THERAPIST: How did you get yourself to keep from taking off, Billy?

BILLY: I didn't want to be grounded.

THERAPIST: OK, but you were willing to risk being grounded before. How did you think about it differently or what did you do differently?

BILLY: I just told myself to go do something else, like play with my baseball cards.

THERAPIST: That's great! How have people reacted to you, now that you've gone a week without running away?

BILLY: They're nice. I got to spend the night at my friend David's house.

MOTHER: Yeah, I knew he was trying hard, so I let him go to David's.

With the "so-so" group, we often have to be persistent in identifying small traces of change. Once we get the ball rolling, as with the "better" group, we can amplify any changes. By redirecting the focus of an adolescent, parent, or other person to change, however small, we can then begin to investigate what other changes may have occurred but weren't so obvious at first.

"Look at What Else Happened . . . "

Sometimes, a parent will have an entirely new concern that was not part of the complaint in the previous session. It is not uncommon for adolescents or parents to move from one problem to another, depending on what transpired on that day or between sessions, or what is looming largely in their mind. In fact, John Weakland used to say, "Life is one damn thing after another." Again, we acknowledge all concerns and do not give short shrift to what people experience. Here's an example of what I typically do in these situations:

During the previous session, Roger's father had voiced his concern over his son's staying out until three or four o'clock in the morning. At the start of the next session, the father related that Roger had skipped school during the week. The therapist acknowledged this concern and then commented, "If it's all right with you, before we talk about this any further, could you give me a brief update on what's happened with the situation of Roger coming in late?"

As discussed throughout this chapter, it's important to check out what has transpired in between sessions. Often, change has occurred but has gone unnoticed. In this particular case, Roger had not been out late all week, and the father's concern had switched. Here's what transpired:

When asked where his concern was, the father replied, "Well, he didn't stay out late this past week, so that's better." To this the therapist responded, "Really? Were you surprised?" "A little," answered the father. The therapist then asked both the father and Roger a series of questions: "Roger, what did you do differently?" "Even though you thought about coming in late a few times, how did you get yourself to come in when you were supposed to?" "What did you do when you found that Roger was coming in on time each night?"

Scaling questions can be helpful, to find out how much progress has been made (Berg & de Shazer, 1993; Berg & Miller, 1992; de Shazer, 1991, 1994; Lipchik, 1988). In the case of Roger, even though he had skipped a day of school, the father felt that things had improved from a five to a six and a half. If the therapist had discussed only the missed day of school, the change might have gone unnoticed.

Even if the problem seems to be resolved, the therapist must make sure that he or she remains in dialogue with the adolescent, family, juvenile officer, teacher, or person, and is clear about what constitutes "better" and when the therapy ought to be terminated. At times, a parent or other person may say something like, "He's gone three weeks before without getting in trouble, but he always does it again." In these situations, the therapist wants to find out how long things would need to go, or what specifically needs to happen, to convince the person that the youth is on the right track and "out of the woods." The following dialogue with a stepfather illustrates this:

STEPFATHER: Well, that's great that he's not fighting at school, but frankly, he's done that before. I mean, he'll do fine for a while and then wham! . . . he's right back at it.

THERAPIST: So he's shown you in the past that he's capable of doing what's he's doing now—staying out of fights. But in the past it doesn't seem like it's lasted. What's the longest that he's gone without fighting?

STEPFATHER: Oh, I guess about eight weeks.

THERAPIST: OK. So how long would he need to go for you to begin to wonder if maybe he was getting the upper hand with fighting and leaving it as part of the past?

STEPFATHER: I think if he went for twelve weeks, then I'd have to say that I'd be pretty convinced. That would be three full months. That would be amazing.

Small increments of change are the target here. In other words, if the stepfather had said, "If he never gets in another fight, then I'll know," we would have to work with him to establish a more reasonable time frame. In these situations, it's often helpful to draw attention to signs of in-between change that indicate movement toward the defined goal or goals. We also want to remember to strive for realistic and attainable change.

COPING SEQUENCE QUESTIONS

Some parents may continue to be pessimistic or cautious about change. They will say, "Yes, but . . . ." As discussed in Chapter 4, at these times it can be useful to ask coping sequence questions (Berg & Gallagher, 1991; Selekman, 1993, 1997). Let's recap these questions:

> *How come things aren't worse with your situation?*
>
> *What have you done to keep things from getting worse?*
>
> *What steps have you taken to prevent things from heading downhill any further?*
>
> *What else has helped to keep things from getting worse?*
>
> *How has that made a difference with your situation?*

Coping sequence questions can help adolescents and family members to orient toward what's working in their lives. Once we find this out, we can begin to explore how their efforts to keep things from getting worse have been helpful in relation to the problem.

SHARING CREDIT FOR CHANGE

If change has occurred with an adolescent and some or all members of a family do not seem to be convinced that it's genuine, it often is because they don't have a sense that they've contributed to the change (Furman & Ahola, 1992). In fact, some family members may even downplay change or attempt to negate it in some way. The reason, in part, may be: if a parent has struggled unsuccessfully to deal with a problem, and then brings a teenager to therapy and things change, the parent can feel further invalidated; a double whammy has been delivered. First, not being able to deal with a son or daughter leaves the parent with a sense of failure. Then, a stranger "fixes" the parent's teenage child.

It is important that therapists attend to this reaction and pass out some accolades when change occurs. Sharing the credit for change can be done in a variety of ways. One tack is to openly give a parent or other person credit: "I'm really impressed with how you instilled in _____ the value of an education." Another is to evoke or elicit, from a parent or other person, something that contributed to the change process. I will sometimes ask: "What part of your parenting do you think contributed most to your son/daughter's ability to overcome _____ ?" A third way is to ask an adolescent: "What did you learn from your parent/guardian/family about how to overcome _____ ?"

When credit for change is shared, a sense of family spirit can often be rekindled. It can be heartwarming to see parents smile, or even shed a tear, when they feel that their contribution is valued.

When Things Are the Same or Worse

Adolescents and families may report, at subsequent sessions, that things are unchanged or worse. For example, a parent might say, "Things certainly aren't any better." Or, "He was even worse this week." When we hear such reports, we want to explore them thoroughly, recalling two things that Sherlock Holmes told Watson: "It is not enough to see. You must also observe." And, "Things are not always as they seem." If we accept clients' negative statements ("Nothing has changed") at face value without further investigation, we run the risk of missing change that may have occurred but has gone unnoticed.

As with the "so-so" group, if a parent or other person begins to heap what appear to be new problems on top of the old ones, we want to gently redirect attention toward what happened in between sessions. Specifically, we want to know how things are in relation to the previously established goals. We can then tackle the new complaints and get an idea of what needs to change and what things will look like when they're better.

If we proceed directly into new complaints without checking to see what has happened in between sessions, we not only might miss change but we also might become overwhelmed. We can become convinced that nothing else is present—only problems. Then, as therapists, our stories about the adolescent or family become problematic. Steve Gilligan (personal communication, 1996) has said that clients will sometimes put therapists into trance by telling compelling stories about how there is nothing else in their lives but problems. They will say, "When you look at me, all you will see is problems. There is nothing else here. Go deeply, go deeply." We want to avoid this induction and not buy into such stories of impossibility.

At times, when parents are upset or frustrated, it can be difficult to wend through their complaints. Two activities seem essential here: (a) continue to make the distinction between stories and experience; and, (b) continue to challenge problematic stories and perceptions while acknowledging what people are experiencing internally. The warmth of acknowledgment and validation can help to melt the frozenness that adolescents and families experience and can allow therapists to open up pathways with possibilities:

Keith was a 17-year-old youth who had been in trouble with the law for repeated substance abuse violations. He had been in drug and alcohol treatment seven times over a span of two years. Each time, he returned to using drugs. He was again referred to therapy after pleading guilty to charges of possession of an illegal substance for the fourth time. During a subsequent session, he said to me, "I'm still using dope. Nothing helps me. It's not getting any better." He was asked how often he was smoking marijuana, at what times, and how much. Through these questions, it was learned that, because Keith had started night school, he wasn't using drugs in the evenings any longer. Usage was mainly in the mornings, to "get him going." This was different in that not only was he not going to school before, but also his drug usage had decreased from several times a day to only in the mornings. In addition, even when he wasn't in school on weekends, he still wasn't using drugs in the evenings! From this information, we were able to find ways for Keith to do things differently in the mornings and continue the change until he was no longer using marijuana.

From Pessimism to Possibility

When reports indicate that things are the same, we can use the coping sequence questions suggested earlier. We can also ask questions that probe more specifically why things have remained as is. We can ask, "What's kept things status quo?" Or, "What's kept things the same?" Then, "What difference has that made for you/your family?"

People who are reporting that things are worse may be, for a variety of reasons, generally pessimistic. At times, joining with an adolescent's or family member's pessimism can be helpful (Berg & Miller, 1992; Selekman, 1993, 1997). We can then ask about what keeps them going, given the problems they are facing. Here are some questions that can be helpful:

What's kept things from bottoming out?

With all that's happened, how have things stayed afloat to any degree?

What keeps you going?

How come you haven't thrown in the towel?

These questions will often provide subtle openings that we can amplify. Once we find an opening, we can follow up with other questions:

What would be the smallest thing that you could do that might make a difference with your situation?

What could others do?

How could we get that to happen a little bit now?

The following excerpt from a case illustrates how to go from a view of pessimism to one of possibility:

STEPFATHER: I don't think we're getting anywhere. We keep coming here but, if anything, I think things are worse.

THERAPIST: It seems to you like things haven't improved yet, and I'm curious, how come things haven't hit rock bottom?

STEPFATHER: I guess because we're willing to keep trying.

THERAPIST: So even though things are tough, your sense is that there is still hope.

STEPFATHER: Oh yeah, there's always hope. It's just hard sometimes.

MOTHER: I agree. We still have hope.

THERAPIST: How has your willingness to keep trying kept things from hitting rock bottom and kept hope alive?

STEPFATHER: That's a good question. I guess we feel like if we just keep trying, eventually there'll be a light at the end of the tunnel and things will improve.

THERAPIST: What would represent a light at the end of the tunnel?

MOTHER: If the fighting and arguing was less.

STEPFATHER: Yeah. The fighting between the kids just drives me crazy.

THERAPIST: OK, so what do you think you or other family members could do that would be a small step toward less fighting and arguing?

STEPFATHER: I think if we all took responsibility for what we say and do.

THERAPIST: What would it take for that to happen?

STEPFATHER: I think if we sat down and had a family meeting. We used to do those, but we stopped when the kids got older.

THERAPIST: That's a great idea. How can you make that happen?

STEPFATHER: I'll just tell everyone they need to be there.

We are not looking for anything momentous here. Instead, when families feel stuck or sense that they are regressing, we want to rekindle some hope and find a pathway that might lead to some small change.

RESTORING AND CREATING RITUALS

Wolin and Wolin (1993) have talked about the importance of maintaining rituals in families where there has been significant dysfunction. One of the findings of their research was that in families where rituals such as eating together, watching a certain television program together, reading stories at bedtime, or other consistent activities were preserved, the children did not develop as many dysfunctional patterns in adulthood. Rituals can be daily, weekly, monthly, seasonal, or annual. They provide a connection with self and others and are a form of prevention against some of the troubles that life presents.

There are at least two ways that we can use rituals. First, as with the case example in the previous section, we can encourage families to restore old rituals that seemed to be helpful in the past. These are called *rituals of continuity* (B. O'Hanlon & Bertolino, 1998):

A grandmother was struggling to take care of her 12-year-old grandson, who had been abandoned by both parents. His behavior was getting the best of her. One evening, the boy said to his grandma, "When we used to come and visit, you would read to me. How come you don't do that anymore?" "I guess because you live here. It's not the same now," replied the woman. "Oh. I didn't know that was going to happen. If I lived somewhere else, would you read to me?" inquired the boy. His grandmother turned to him and said, "I didn't know you liked it so much. You don't have to live somewhere else for us to have 'storytime,' and besides, no one can tell stories like me!" The two were able to restore their standing appointment for storytime, which was held each evening at 8:30 P.M.

A second way is to help families create new *rituals of connection* (B. O'Hanlon & Bertolino, 1998). Family members may have transitioned to different places in the family life cycle (Carter & McGoldrick, 1989). Thus, their needs and their patterns of interaction may have changed. With rituals of connection, we want to prescribe something that restores or makes connections to people or situations:

David and his father had always been close. Since he was 7 years old, David would follow his dad around the house as he worked, and the two would spend lots of time together. It seemed that they always found time for each other. As time passed and things changed, David spent more and more time with his friends. As their relationship began to become more estranged, David's father sensed that his son only wanted to hang out with kids his age and had lost interest in him. Their times together became but a memory.

Around the time he turned 16, David began to find trouble. He was caught stealing; then came a breaking and entering charge. His father's heart was broken; he felt there was something he should have done. But he could only watch. Finally, a third conviction sent David to a juvenile facility.

After some time, David was able to go out on weekend passes. One hot and muggy August weekend, David's father picked him up from the juvenile facility. As they were driving along, his father, ever so apprehensively, pulled out a pair of baseball tickets. He said to his son, "I'm sure you want to see your friends because you don't get to come home much, but I figured I'd ask anyway. Do you want to go to this game?" As his father handed him the tickets, David began to cry. He said, "I didn't think you'd ever want to be around me again after what I'd done." "I didn't think you would ever want to be around me again because I wasn't cool anymore," responded his father. The two went on to share a few laughs and tears together. Four years later, David and his father are committed season ticket holders who look forward to their time together.

STILL STUCK!

When adolescents and families still seem to be stuck, it can be useful to consider some of the ideas offered in previous chapters. Here are some possibilities:

1. Try changing patterns of attention.
2. Use pattern intervention.
3. Try the Do Something Different task, and encourage creativity.
4. Externalize the problem.
5. Use a reflecting team.
6. Try the KidsCan approach.
7. Offer stories, metaphors, and other anecdotes.

Alan Watts (1966) once said, "Problems that remain persistently insolvable should always be suspected as questions asked the wrong way" (p. 55). With this in mind, and in order to generate other ideas, it can be helpful to consult with colleagues from various other theoretical orientations. A possibility therapy approach hinges on the dissolution of theoretical boundaries. Thus, let's consider how various ideas can fit together to ultimately benefit youth and families.

STRENGTHENING THE VALUED STORY

When change has occurred, I have found it important to strengthen the valued and preferred story about the adolescent. In this section, I outline several ways of doing this. They include using *letters, certificates,* and *letters of evidence.*

Letters That Stand the Test of Time

Letters from therapists can be useful in amplifying change, reinforcing ideas discussed in therapy, highlighting exceptions, and opening up further possibilities (Friedman, 1997; White & Epston, 1990). Letters can be used after one session, after twelve sessions, at the end of therapy, or whenever a clinician thinks they might be helpful. In a recent survey, Nylund and Thomas (1994) found that "the average worth of a letter was 3.2 face-to-face interviews" (p. 39). David Epston (in White, 1995) related that his clients have reported that letters are worth an average of 4.5 sessions. In the Nylund and Thomas study, some of the participants even indicated that letters were worth as much as ten sessions! The study also found that over 50% of the participants attributed the change made in therapy to the letters alone.

Letters are a form of communication that stays with adolescents and families. Because they can be read and reread, they often become ongoing sources of support. Here are two sample letters, one to an adolescent client and one to a family.

Letters can be written to individuals, couples, or entire families. They are a good way of highlighting changes that have occurred or might occur in the future. Letters generally speak to

Dear James,

I wanted to drop you a brief note to share some thoughts with you.

At the start of therapy you mentioned that last school year was a tough one. You had a hard time keeping up with your studies and getting your homework handed in, and that hurt you when it came time to play football. But this year was different. You started off summer school with a bang and used your pre-season well to prepare for the regular season. Now that you're on a roll, I wonder how good a shape you'll be in when the regular season starts in the fall. It seems that you've got some momentum going now.

I keep wondering how you're going to use the new learnings you described to me. I hope that you will let me know somehow. It's exciting to think that I may be reading about both your academic and sports achievements in the newspaper! Keep me posted!

Sincerely,

Bob Bertolino, PhD

preferred futures or a way of being for adolescents and families. Many styles and messages can be conveyed in written letters, and the flexibility of the format allows the therapist to be creative.

Certifiably Changed

When an adolescent has accomplished change in regard to a problem or in the area of a problem, one way to help solidify the change is to present a certificate. This is not a new idea; teachers, scout leaders, and others have given awards for years. Certificates can be awarded for overcoming specific or general problems. For example, if a youth has been having trouble with his or her temper, he or she might be given a certificate stating that "bad tempers" or

Dear Mr. and Mrs. Richards, Doug, and Beth,

I am writing to share with you a few thoughts that I've had since our last meeting.

I was so impressed with the commitment that each of you was willing to make to solve your problem of family chaos. That was also very heartwarming to me. You're facing changes that can sometimes cause friction in families and often require creative thinking.

Mr. Richards, I have to wonder what creative juices may be with you, given your experience as a lawyer. Mrs. Richards, as a teacher, you mentioned that you deal with chaos every day. I wonder how your experience with chaos will come into play. Doug, being 16 years old, you're now closer to being an adult than a child. I can't help but be curious as to what ideas you'll have. And Beth, now that you've moved into the teenage years, you probably have a new perspective on things. I wonder what you'll come up with to help lessen the chaos.

I left the session wondering what was going to be the next step for each of you and also for the family as a whole. I'll be curious to hear about what's transpired between now and the next time we meet. I look forward to seeing you on _____.

Sincerely,

Bob Bertolino, PhD

"Ms. Temper's" advances had been overcome. In other instances, a youth may be given a certificate for standing up to "juvenile delinquency."

A playful way to do a certificate is to have the adolescent and family come up with a name that suits the problem. This nickname can inject a bit of humor and make the certificate more personalized. Figures 6.1 and 6.2 offer examples of certificates that represent change.

Tantrum Tamer Certificate

This certificate is hereby awarded to

Gary Thomas

On this day, December 3rd, 1999
For demonstrating his ability to tame tantrums

Robert Bertolino
Robert Bertolino, Ph.D.

FIGURE 6.1   Tantrum Tamer Certificate.

The Evidence Is Mounting

I frequently suggest to youth that they collect "evidence" of their change: report cards, completed and graded assignments, teacher progress reports, pay stubs from a job, parental notes identifying improved behavior, juvenile officer reports, newspaper clippings, and so

---

Certificate of Change

This certificate is hereby awarded to

Laurie Waters

On this day, December 3rd, 1999
For success in standing up to juvenile delinquency
And
Getting her life back

Robert Bertolino
Robert Bertolino, Ph.D.

FIGURE 6.2   Certificate of Change.

on (Bertolino, 1998a). I've used this idea in two ways: to create "Official Letters of Evidence" (Figure 6.3), and to combine the letters with an "Evidence Log" (Figure 6.4).

Letters of evidence represent specific instances of change that are noticeable by others. Parents, teachers, juvenile officers, coaches, or others who have noticed positive change in a youth can fill out and sign these letters. I usually suggest that several copies be provided to those persons who might notice change. This can make the delivery of letters of evidence more spontaneous. Interestingly, if there is

---

OFFICIAL
LETTER OF EVIDENCE

Name: _____

Week of: _____

Type of Evidence Reviewed:

_____
_____
_____
_____
_____
_____
_____
_____

Verified by: _____
Date: _____

FIGURE 6.3   Official Letter of Evidence.

MY EVIDENCE LOG

NAME: _____

WEEK OF: _____

☺ 1.

☺ 2.

☺ 3.

☺ 4.

☺ 5.

FIGURE 6.4   My Evidence Log.

apprehension on the part of one of these people, the use of letters of evidence can help to reorient that person's attention from problems to possibilities.

Evidence logs are then used to track the various forms of evidence that have been gathered. For example, a youth may have one piece of evidence from a juvenile officer, one from a teacher, and one from a parent. Evidence that is obtained and recorded can play a significant role in the changing of an adolescent's self-story.

A second way of tracking change is to have adolescents come up with their own creations. Here's how I typically introduce this to youth:

Down the road, others may be curious as to how you managed to get the upper hand with _____ [fill in the blank]. I'm wondering, sometimes kids or teenagers have scrapbooks, diaries, or other ways of keeping track of their accomplishments. I'm curious as to how you will be keeping track of your struggle with _____ [fill in the blank]. What are some ideas that might work for you?

Youth are asked to store the information they have gathered, as a way of preserving the change (Bertolino, 1998a). Some compile scrapbooks, design posters, or make collages. Others create charts or use diaries, journals, or books. In any case, adolescents get a chance to be as creative as they wish. Their projects stand as representatives of change. With both activities, initially, "hints" of change may be more the norm. These are smaller bits of evidence that are signs of a more significant future change (i.e., passing a test, being in on time for a week, and so on).

Sharing Change with Larger Audiences

Good news about youth (i.e., honor roll, academic achievements, sports successes, community efforts, and so on) appears in newspapers and other media every day. Thus, the accomplishments of adolescents are often highlighted in other contexts—an idea that can also be applied to youth who have overcome difficulties. That is, by sharing change with a larger social context, the valued story of an adolescent can be strengthened (Freedman & Combs, 1996). Freeman, Epston, and Lobovits (1997) remarked, "The process of gathering information to share with others invites a further 'performance of meaning,' thereby strengthening the narrative" (p. 125). For some adolescents, placing their change in a broader social context seems to *historicize* or solidify it in some way.

I have used this idea in three ways. First, a few moments ago, I discussed how adolescents can be asked to collect evidence in a variety of forms. Often, they are thrilled to show their collections of evidence to family members, teachers, or others. I encourage this practice. When I have used this idea, the scrapbook/collage/poster has often ended up looking like a "collection of competence." It becomes a representation of an adolescent's accomplishments and change.

A second way to place change in a larger social context is to ask the youth to be a consultant to others with similar problems. Freeman et al. (1997) wrote that when a child, in their example, has taken significant steps toward revising his or her relationship with a problem, he or she "has gained knowledge and expertise that may assist others grappling with similar concerns" (p. 126). With parental consent, youth and/or families can be audiotaped or videotaped describing how they managed to overcome their problem. These tapes can then be played for other adolescents and families. Youth can also attend therapy sessions and serve as consultants to other youth. This not only can help to strengthen a youth's sense of self but also can help other families who are stuck.

A final way is to ask youth to volunteer with local youth organizations. Where I am employed, we have a "Peer Partner" program: youth volunteers assist other youth who are in our programs. They provide conversation, companionship, support, and, often, invaluable ideas to other adolescents. Many former clients have become peer partners and we consider the program to be as important as any others that we run.

This chapter has offered a myriad of ideas for working with adolescents and families in second and subsequent sessions. In addition, ways of solidifying change have been outlined. The next chapter discusses the importance of accountability, as well as how to work collaboratively with youth and families when psychiatric labels and psychotropic medications have been instituted. I'll also talk about mandated clients and larger systems.

CHAPTER SEVEN

*Encompassing Angles
with Circles*

CONVERSATIONS FOR
ACCOUNTABILITY AND CHANGE

*I am only one. But still, I am one. I cannot do everything,
but still I can do something. And because I cannot do
everything, I will not refuse to do the something that I
can do.*

—Edward Everett Hale

A 14-YEAR-OLD FEMALE WAS *mandated to attend counseling after she assaulted a police officer and was disruptive at school. When I contacted her mother, she remarked that her daughter was fine and did not need counseling "just because she was pregnant." I assured her that the referral was not for the pregnancy concern but for the reasons just mentioned. Despite her apprehension, the mother finally agreed to an appointment a week later.*

When she entered the office with her daughter, the mother stated, "This is crap; those people at the court can go to hell and you can go there too if you think you can counsel my daughter because she's pregnant! You're a man so you can't even know what being pregnant is about!" I again assured her that the reason for the referral was the charges of assault against her daughter. However, she continued to verbally express herself and explained that she had an infection and if she fell outside she would sue the agency, me, and the court because she had to attend therapy. She stated, "I've had to listen to those idiots at the court and their shit, and if you think I'm gonna listen to your shit, you've got another think coming!"

After the mother uttered a few more profanities, I responded to her, "You can be as upset as you need to be. You have every right to your feelings, and at the same time it's not OK for you to say nasty things to me. Now, I'm very sorry that you don't feel well, and I'll do what I can to get you on your way as soon as possible."

I proceeded to see the daughter individually for about twenty minutes, during which time the mother, still angry, left the room to call the juvenile officer and express her opinions. At the end of the session, she reentered the office. I then spoke with both of them. "I can see that you both have a lot going on, and I certainly don't want to pile more on top of it. It's OK if you're mad at me and the court or whoever, and I'm sorry that you don't feel well. The situation is that your daughter has had some trouble recently, and this counseling may or may not help. I'm optimistic that it can. But I'm not going to fight with you or even have you make a decision at this point. Here's the situation I'd like you to consider—you can decide to come back and we will work together to try and get things on track, or you can decide not to come back." The mother responded, "If we don't come back, you'll tell her DJO that we're bad and resisting therapy." I replied, "I will contact the DJO, but I will only tell her that your decision was to not return. You can then have that other conversation with her."

I asked the mother and daughter to go home and think about what they wanted to do, and to call in a day or two with their answer. Twenty minutes after they had left, the mother called, "I owe you an apology for the way I acted. I'm very sorry. I was way out of line and if it's all right I'd like to set up another appointment. And if it's OK, could I bring my stepson? He's been having trouble too."

This woman was extremely upset for a variety of reasons. All of what she was experiencing was OK. Not all of her actions were OK. While I acknowledged and validated her, it was also important to hold her accountable for what she was doing wrong—in this case, what she was saying. This is not always easy with adolescents and families; conversations can quickly become explosive. This chapter delves into areas that tend to be controversial and heated, among adolescents, family members, and outside helpers.

First, I'll discuss some specific ways of promoting accountability with adolescents *and* parents. This will be followed by ideas for working with adolescents who have been given psychiatric labels and psychotropic medications. Working with mandated youth and within larger systems is the final topic. Each of these areas will be explored to clarify how mental health professionals can maintain a collaborative position with youth, families, and outside helpers, and find a fit with what are often perceived as opposing paradigms.

ACCOUNTABILITY

Accountability can be a major consideration when working with adolescents and families. I say "can" because, with many families, we won't need to bring it up. In other cases, therapists will have to clarify areas of accountability with both adolescents *and* parents. I will talk about accountability in two particular ways here: (a) how therapists can convey what it is that each person is accountable for, and (b) how therapists can talk with adolescents, family members, and others in a way that invites accountability. Let's explore these one at a time.

A Sign of the Times: Accountability Is Not a Choice

Adolescents and parents/guardians/caregivers are responsible and accountable for different things. In all cases, adolescents should be held accountable for their actions and behaviors; however, extra attention is sometimes needed in this area. Parents and adults who are in the position of caretakers should also be held accountable for their behaviors and actions, including looking after their children. Most states have laws regarding the responsibilities of caregivers for the whereabouts of youth.

Let's get specific. Parents will sometimes say things such as, "He does whatever he wants, whenever he wants," or, "I don't have any control over her." In most states, if a youth is away from home without permission, the parent or caretaker can contact the police and file an absence report. Parents, legal guardians, or caretakers who do not report a runaway can be held responsible, and in some cases, criminally charged. Many new laws have been instituted in response to the high number of missing children. There have been cases of parents' being charged with criminal neglect because they did not report that their son or daughter was missing.

Some parents will ride out an absence because they do not want to get their kids in trouble. It is up to the therapist to work with parents and help them to understand the implications of failing to report (their children could get hurt, be hurting someone else, committing crimes, and so on). It is equally important that adolescents understand this process and know that their parent will be contacting the proper authorities if they choose to run away, break curfew, or commit a crime. Here's a dialogue I had with a father and his son regarding their respective responsibilities:

THERAPIST: So Jeff has run away three times in the last ten days?

FATHER: Right, and he may have snuck out a couple of other times—I'm not sure.

JEFF: It's not running away, dad! I'm just outside, a few blocks away. You act like I'm a criminal!

THERAPIST: You're not a criminal, Jeff. At the same time, taking off—which is called running away by the police because you're not where you're supposed to be according to your dad—is an offense. Do you know what I mean?

JEFF: Not really.

THERAPIST: Well, your dad is responsible for knowing where you are. If he just let you run the streets and didn't care, and you got hurt, or somebody else did, or you committed a crime, the police could come back to your dad and say, "Why didn't you report that your son was missing?" It's also possible that Children's Services could get involved for your dad's not reporting that you were gone. These types of things are taken seriously because there are so many missing children and teenagers. *(to the father)* OK. So what do you usually do when he leaves?

FATHER: Well, I usually wait until he comes back. Then I ground him or whatever.

THERAPIST: How has that worked?

FATHER: It hasn't.

THERAPIST: What I'm going to ask of you is that the next time he runs away, you report it. It's your responsibility. It's his choice to leave. He can make that decision for himself. But it's your responsibility to let the authorities know when he leaves—unless of course he's in your yard and you can see him—then he's on your property. Same thing if he's real late or breaks curfew. And it's important that you do this every time, not just once in a while. Can you do that?

FATHER: Sure. I didn't know I could just call the police.

THERAPIST: You can. Sometimes they will come by and take a report and sometimes you can just call them and they'll do one over the phone. You'll have to check with your local police department to see what their protocol is. Does that make sense?

FATHER: Yeah.

THERAPIST: Jeff, I've asked your dad to do this because that's his job. When he does it, it's not because he's being mean; it's because that's what he has to do as a father and a law-abiding citizen. You're capable of deciding for yourself what's the best decision, and he's just going to do his job.

FATHER: So what if I keep reporting him leaving and he still does it?

THERAPIST: That's another reason for this too. Many times, kids will find themselves in a lot of trouble and parents won't know what to do. Their son or daughter will have run away a bunch of times and they'll call the juvenile authorities and they'll say, "We're sorry, but we don't have any record of your son running away. Did you report the runaways?" At that point, the parent will have no recourse as far as the court goes. However, if the runaways or curfew violations have been reported, the court has something they can take action on.

FATHER: I got it. I know someone that happened to.

Laws regarding running away, curfew violation, and truancy vary from state to state, and it is up to mental health professionals to become educated on their content. Conversations similar to the one above can also be applied to situations involving property damage, assault, and other crimes. It is up to parents and caregivers to report these offenses and press charges. Just as it's not OK for a person to go into someone else's house and cause damage or be assaultive, it's not OK for those things to happen at home.

Invitations to Accountability

In Chapter 3, I discussed how stories can become problematic. When working with adolescents, therapists have to be aware of stories of nonaccountability, nonchoice, and determinism. For example, youth or parents will sometimes attempt to explain or justify a behavior by attributing it to a genetic, developmental, interpersonal, personality, or other propensity. A parent might say, "He's ADHD. He can't help it." We don't want to buy into these kinds of stories. Instead, we want to begin to invite youth and families into accountability. Let's explore three ways to do this.

1. *Reflect back nonaccountability statements without the nonaccountability part.* When adolescents use an excuse or explanation, therapists can repeat back the statement but drop the nonaccountability part. Here's how to do this:

Adolescent: He was looking at me weird, so I hit him.

Therapist: You hit him.

Adolescent: She yelled at me, so I took off.

Therapist: You ran away.

Adolescent: He's always making me mad. That's why I kicked a hole in the wall.

Therapist: You kicked a hole in the wall.

2. *Find counterexamples that indicate choice or accountability.* Another way to invite accountability is to search for exceptions to the behavior or action for which a youth is claiming he or she isn't accountable. We can often make generalizations here because it is impossible for an adolescent to do negative behavior 24 hours a day (although some parents would beg to differ!). Here's how to do this:

Adolescent: I can't help it. My mom hit me when I was little, so that's the only way I know to handle my anger.

Therapist: I'm curious, though; you got angry with your teacher yesterday and you didn't hit her. How did that happen?

Adolescent: If she yells at me, she knows I'm gonna take off.

Therapist: How come you don't take off every time you think she's yelling at you?

Adolescent: She's just gonna give me a bad grade, so why should I do my homework?

Therapist: I must be missing something. How did you manage to get some passing grades on your homework at the beginning of the semester?

3. *Use the word "and" to link together internal experience and accountability.* As has been a theme throughout this book, all internal experience is OK but not all actions are OK. Thus, it can be helpful to reflect back what an adolescent or other person is experiencing internally, and link it with that for which he or she is accountable. To do this, we use the word "and" as opposed to "but." In the opening

story of this chapter, I did this by saying to the mother, "You can be as upset as you need to be. You have every right to your feelings, and at the same time it's not OK for you to say nasty things to me." Here are some more examples:

ADOLESCENT: She always makes me so mad that I hit her!

THERAPIST: You can be as mad as you need to be, and it's not OK to hit her.

ADOLESCENT: I can't help it! I just can't stop it!

THERAPIST: You can feel like you can't help it, and you can help it and stop it.

ADOLESCENT: If he just wouldn't say anything to me, I wouldn't have to run away.

THERAPIST: It's OK to feel like you've got to take off, and it's not OK to run away.

Too often, adolescents get the message that they shouldn't feel the way they do or that they are overreacting. That message can be extremely invalidating. These three simple techniques can be very useful in diffusing emotional reactivity and simultaneously promoting accountability.

WHO'S DRIVING THE BUS? CONSTRUCTIONS OF HELP AND HARM

Working with Psychiatric Labels

In today's mental health care environment, the role of psychiatric diagnoses for adolescents is a primary concern for families and therapists. For families, diagnoses are often needed in order to qualify for counseling services. For therapists, it is generally necessary to file insurance claims and to collect third-party payments. There are staunch advocates on each side of the argument as to whether psychiatric labeling is harmful or helpful. I see the labeling as something that we must contend with, like it or not. Until the climate changes, we must find ways of coexisting with diagnostic labels.

Let's consider how labels can be harmful and helpful in working with adolescents.

Labels can be validating when they provide people with a sense that they are not alone—other people are suffering similar difficulties or adversity. Bill O'Hanlon tells a story about how he ran an advertisement in a local newspaper, looking for people to attend a group therapy he was doing (in Hoyt, 1996b). The group was to consist of people who would eat too much and then make themselves throw up. The response to his ad was overwhelming. Some of the people who called were even tearful; they couldn't believe that others did the same thing.

At the time that Bill ran his group, there was no such label as bulimia, but there were people who experienced similar symptoms. Once a diagnostic category was constructed, it gave many people, mainly women, the sense that they weren't alone. The creation of the label also led to further research in the area of eating disorders.

For parents who are frustrated and are blaming themselves, labels can let them know that they're not alone. Some labels even have brought people together. For example, just as there are support groups for parents who have lost children, there are now support groups for parents whose children have been diagnosed with a variety of psychiatric disorders. I have met many parents who have found these types of groups to be extremely helpful. Again, the classification of symptoms into diagnoses has led to further research into finding more effective therapeutic approaches.

On the other side of the debate, labels can unnecessarily categorize and stigmatize youth and families (Sowell, 1997). Once given a label, an adolescent can find himself or herself in a situation where parents, teachers, school officials, court representatives, and others cannot separate the youth from the diagnosis. In a sense, the youth becomes the diagnosis. Further, because obtaining an accurate diagnosis for an adolescent is not a simple task, it is not uncommon for mental health professionals to give a wrong diagnosis. But once labeled, it can be hard to remove the stigma. Thus, diagnoses can cause significant distress within families and can sometimes lead to the loss of hope.

What happens when we have to give a diagnosis and we are working from a possibility therapy perspective? Again, as with required assessment procedures, these seemingly dichotomous approaches can coexist. We want to remain collaborative and explain the process to youth and parents. We say, "In order for the insurance company to pay for the therapy, I have to turn in a diagnosis." Or, "It's a requirement of this agency that I assign a diagnosis." The therapist can then work with the family to come up with the least stigmatizing diagnosis that simultaneously fits the complaint.

When more than one adolescent is present, or when there are children of varying ages, it may be necessary to say to the family, "Someone will have to be the person who gets the diagnosis here. Who is willing to be that person?" The idea is: The diagnosis should not be taboo, and the therapist should involve the family with the label, as with every other aspect of the therapy.

Even when a diagnosis is necessary, it is important for the therapist to remain clear on what the problem is (in action-based language) and how it will be known when things are better. It is equally important that he or she continues to promote accountability throughout the therapy. A psychiatric diagnosis does not remove accountability.

We have to remember that psychiatric diagnoses are social constructions. They are explanations. As discussed in an earlier chapter, diagnoses are much harder to work with than well-defined problematic behaviors. Because a possibility therapy approach is client-driven, we are not interested in treating theoretical constructions. We treat only client-defined problems.

WATCHING OUR WORDS: FROM LIABILITY TO ABILITY

Sometimes, therapists encounter "therapy veterans" who have mastered the use of psychological jargon. With these persons, it's usually helpful for the therapist to begin to shift the language so that a different, less stigmatizing perspective can be offered. This can give families a sense of hope and shift the focus of therapy from inability to ability. For example, if a mother describes her son as "hyperactive," we might suggest that he's "full of energy." Or, a youth labeled as "narcissistic" might be described as "independent." Further, if a teenager is referred to as "manipulative," we might offer that he or she is "creative."

As therapists, we want to use language to cocreate solvable problems. Even when family members enter therapy using jargon, we can offer other ways of talking that are less pathological. The wrong language can be like a virus. How therapists talk about problems, possibilities, and solutions will in some way influence how clients talk about their concerns and problems.

Psychotropic Medications: Playing the Percentages

At an alarming rate, adolescents are being placed on various psychotropic medications for the treatment of psychiatric diagnoses such as ADD/ADHD, Oppositional Defiant Disorder, Conduct Disorder, as well as many others (American Psychiatric Association, 1994). A recent review of research has called this practice into question by suggesting that such a trend in unethical, ineffective, and potentially dangerous (Fisher & Fisher, 1997). This should be a principal concern of all therapists, regardless of their theoretical orientations. The well-being of adolescents and children must never be compromised.

If medications are prescribed, I always make sure that parents are as well informed as possible. This means talking with their child's psychiatrist and understanding what the medication is *supposed* to do. They should know what side effects to look for, and how to monitor those side effects. I view medication as a viable option for some youth. My concern is that family members become educated on psychotropic medications and understand as clearly as possible, what the pros and cons may be.

Unfortunately, with adolescents and parents, what is often associated with the prescription of psychotropic drugs is a sense that the medication itself is in charge; that is, without the medication, the youth is "out of control" or "can't control" his or her behavior and actions. Such a message provides excuses for adolescents and parents and removes personal agency. As therapists, it is important that we continue to hold youth accountable whether on medication or not. As discussed earlier, we can invite youth into conversations where they assume accountability. Here are some examples of how to do this:

ADOLESCENT: My mom forgot to give me my medication, so I couldn't help it. I hit him.

THERAPIST: You hit him.

ADOLESCENT: I've been taking medicine for my anger since I was six years old. If I don't get it, I can't sit still.

THERAPIST: I'm curious. Your mom mentioned to me that you don't take medication on weekends because you're not in school. She also said that you can play video games for hours on the weekend. How do you manage to sit still for so long on weekends without your medication?

ADOLESCENT: If I don't get my medication on time, I know I'll lose control.

THERAPIST: You can feel like you can't control yourself without your medication, and you can still control yourself.

Another way of inviting adolescents who are on medication into accountability is to find out from them what percentage of their desired behavior is due to their being "in charge of" as opposed to being "ruled by" the medication. Here's a recent dialogue I had with an adolescent about this:

BLAIR: My medication calms me down and so I don't fight.

THERAPIST: It makes you feel calmer. Is that right?

BLAIR: Yeah.

THERAPIST: So when you're able to hold back from fighting, what do you do?

BLAIR: Well, I just don't do it. I walk away.

THERAPIST: How do you get yourself to do that?

BLAIR: I just tell myself not to fight.

THERAPIST: You know, I haven't come across a medication yet that makes decisions for people. In your case, what percentage of your holding back from fighting is because of you, and what percentage is due to the medication?

BLAIR: I guess 75% me and 25% medication.

THERAPIST: What does that 75% of you do to help you make good decisions and keep you from fighting?

BLAIR: I just know that I have to make good decisions; otherwise, I'll be in big trouble—so I do whatever I have to do to not fight.

We are aiming to help the adolescents gain a sense that they are making decisions, not the medication. The medication may be contributing to how they feel, but no medication makes decisions or is a source of control to youth. We want to promote accountability and invite and empower adolescents to have an improved sense of personal agency.

WORKING WITH MANDATED ADOLESCENTS

Clear Expectations

Mandated youth can be referred by a variety of sources, including court systems, police officers, protective service agencies, school officials, and other concerned adults. Although these cases frequently involve at least one person who is only trying to get out of coming to therapy, most research indicates that mandated clients fare just as well as those who are not mandated to attend therapy (Tohn & Oshlag, 1996). This has also been my experience in working with both voluntary and involuntary adolescents.

It is particularly important to establish a connection with adolescents. To do this, I tell stories, use humor, and inquire about their interests and lives. I let adolescents know that my job is not to make their life miserable, but to help get them to where they want to be tomorrow, next week, month, year, or whenever their desired future may begin. I also explain to youth that therapy *can be brief,* and what they have to say and what they do will influence the length of treatment.

I want to be clear with adolescents about the limits of confidentiality. There are laws about reporting abuse and neglect. There are issues related to duty to warn and the risk of suicide. Other considerations are professional ethics codes and state licensing requirements. There may also be extenuating circumstances, such as having to report to the referring body. Thus, a clear and thorough statement of confidentiality is necessary.

Educating as Opposed to Confronting Adolescents

With court-referred cases, I will sometimes offer a brief commentary on how things work within the court system. Truly, many youth *and* parents do not know what could happen if there continues to be trouble. I do not say, "If you keep getting into trouble, you'll be locked up." Or, "You'd better think twice about what you're doing!" I simply offer them a brief summary, and they can decide what to do with the information. Here's how I typically do this:

I'm not sure if you know how the court process works or not. But I like to give people a brief rundown so that they have the information they need to make good decisions. You may already know some of this, and that's OK. You can just tune into what you think is important for you.

When a youth under 18 gets into trouble and a police report is filed, a copy automatically gets sent to the family court. Then, the people at the court have to decide whether they're going to do anything or not. Sometimes they do and sometimes they don't. It usually depends on how many reports are already on file on the teenager. If they decide to do something, they can proceed either to an informal or a formal hearing. An informal hearing means that you go in and talk with a juvenile officer. A formal hearing means that you go before a judge.

There are lots of things the court can do. They can just talk to you about what's happened. They can send you to classes such as "Street Law" or to therapy. They can also put you into the detention center until they decide what to do. There's also informal or formal probation. The last step is usually placement in one of the court-contracted facilities, or commitment to the Division of Youth Services for residential placement. As you may or may not know, placement is nothing like home and I wouldn't wish it upon anyone.

Now, here's the great part to all this. You have say-so in what happens to you right now. I may or may not be able to say that down the road. But as things stand today, your actions from here forward will determine what happens to you in the eyes of the court. I have no idea what you're going to do with the information I just offered you. But at the very least, I'm sure you'll tell your friends about how the court system works so they'll be as informed as you are. I'm looking forward to seeing how you meet the challenge.

I maintain a nonconfrontational, collaborative approach in delivering this information. I do not lecture. In turn, it seems to me that adolescents and parents do listen and do not tune me out. They also ask a lot of very important questions, and I can either verify or dispel any myths that they've heard. I think it's good to *offer* information and educate youth in a way that is not confrontational. Because local, county, and state laws differ, mental health professionals should find out how the court systems in their areas operate, so they can pass on accurate information.

Filing Reports

I inform court-referred youth that I will be talking with their juvenile officers about their cases. And, when reports are prepared, they will have the opportunity to contribute their opinions to what is written. Thus, reports are based on conversations with both the adolescent and his or her parent or legal guardian. Even this aspect of therapy remains collaborative. The following case example illustrates how collaborative reports can be written with adolescents, to facilitate the therapy process:

A supervisee of mine had a case of a 12-year-old girl who was mandated into a "tracker"—a case management type of program. She had missed twenty of the first fifty-five days of school. In preparing his monthly summary for the court, it was necessary for him to write down how much school she had missed. Because the girl was always very curious as to what went into the monthly summaries and often didn't like what they had to say about her, it was suggested that the supervisee collaborate more with her. I suggested that he say to her, "Up until now, you've been attending school about 64% of the time. What needs to happen so that when you and I do the report next month, it says that you've been going at least 80% of the time?" It was also suggested that he ask for any ideas that she might have for things she could do during the next month, which then could be included in the next month's report.

In my experience, collaborating with youth throughout the entire process of therapy facilitates change. Further, the fact that an adolescent is mandated to attend therapy does not mean that the therapy will be tougher or less successful.

WORKING WITH LARGER SYSTEMS

Collaborating with Outside Helpers: Mirroring What We've Already Learned

Working with adolescents requires that therapists routinely collaborate with outside helpers. These can include juvenile officers, teachers, school officials, social service agencies, and a host of others. This task can be very challenging because there are often distinctly different ideas about what should happen with any particular case. Frequently, outside helpers have already made up their minds about how youth are or will be in the future, and may have written them off. I sometimes have to begin by creating the sense that things can change:

A juvenile officer contacted me and said, "This kid needs to be rehabilitated. He's a habitual and chronic offender. He's got a poor prognosis for the future. I'm gonna send him to see you, but that's just to try and keep him from getting worse. I need time to find a placement." I inquired, "What if he doesn't get into any trouble while you're searching for a placement? Will you consider other alternatives?" To this she responded, "I'd consider it, but this kid hasn't gone for more than a few weeks without doing something. It would be a minor miracle for him to not get into some kind of trouble." "Maybe it won't take a miracle," I replied. "We'll see," she chirped.

After gaining a small opening with the juvenile officer, I was able to find out what her biggest complaint was and how she would know when the adolescent was doing better. Does this sound familiar? This is the same approach that we take with clients. We want to know what the problem is in action-based terms, and how they will know when things are better. Here's an edited excerpt of how I went about using this process with the deputy juvenile officer (DJO):

THERAPIST: So that I'm clear here, what specifically do you think is the most important thing for me to address in therapy?

DJO: Definitely his attitude about things. He thinks he's invincible.

THERAPIST: So what has he done that gives you the sense that he thinks he's invincible?

DJO: He's assaulted people and has stolen and doesn't think he'll get caught for it even though he has [been caught] many times.

THERAPIST: So what would start to convince you that he wasn't seeing himself as being invincible any longer and maybe more human?

DJO: He'd have to not assault people and steal, for one. He'd also have to talk more respectfully to me. He tries to intimidate me.

THERAPIST: OK. So if he wasn't assaulting people, he stopped stealing, and he was more respectful in how he talked with you, then you'd have to wonder if maybe he was turning things around?

DJO: Oh yeah, but I can't see it happening.

THERAPIST: So it would be surprising to you?

DJO: Definitely.

THERAPIST: And just for clarity's sake, if he did those things, you would reconsider whether residential treatment was the right place for him or not?

DJO: That's right.

Whether working with juvenile officers, teachers, social service workers, or other outside helpers, we want to be clear on what their expectations are in each case. If what outside helpers expect seems unreasonable, then we will want to do just as we do with clients: work to cocreate realistic and achievable goals while preserving accountability.

When outside helpers are involved, their presence or involvement should be incorporated into therapy sessions. I usually do this in two ways. First, I ask a youth, "Did your DJO tell you what he or she expects us to talk about in therapy?" If the youth or parent knows, then we can proceed. If not, I will ask a youth to speculate: "What do you think it will take for your DJO to be convinced that you no longer need to come here?"

If a youth or parent doesn't know, then I use the second approach. If I've already talked with the outside helper, I offer what I've learned from talking with him or her. If not, I contact the outside helper in between sessions and, at the next therapy appointment, I introduce my understandings. I will say something like, "From what I understand, when you _____ , then your DJO will get the sense that you're moving in the right direction." I then follow with, "How does that sound to you?" And, "What do you think would be a first step in that direction?"

Incorporating Outside Helpers into Sessions

Outside helpers can also be invited to attend therapy sessions. Multiple viewpoints can be especially helpful when adolescents and families are stuck. Often, such meetings can foster new possibilities and solutions. In addition, by adding new members to sessions, sometimes the "not yet said" (Anderson & Goolishian, 1988), which is usually a piece of new information or a new view, is offered. This new information may be the missing piece of a puzzle, or new pathways of possibility that had gone unexplored.

When outside helpers join therapy sessions, we want to remember that there are many ways to view a situation and no one view is more correct than another. At the same time, we want to challenge perspectives that close down the possibilities of change. Our goal is to promote change.

CHAPTER EIGHT

From End to Beginning

THE CASE OF RICHARD

Become what you are.

—Alan Watts

A s a way of bringing together the ideas presented in this book, I present here an entire case. The dialogue has been edited and is interspersed with commentary to highlight some of the ideas offered in other chapters.

Richard was a 14-year-old Caucasian male who was referred to therapy after multiple offenses. He had experienced bouts of truancy, violation of curfew, running away, and assaultive behavior. He was placed on probation because of these infractions, and was on the verge of being placed residentially at the time of therapy. The transcripts have been edited but they represent five sequential sessions with Richard and his mother, Laura. I have interspersed commentary to highlight various ideas that have been offered throughout this book.

SESSION ONE

Bob: So where would you like to start?

Richard: I had to come. My DJO [Deputy Juvenile Officer] told me if I didn't, she'd put me back in juvy. I didn't have a choice.

[I've discussed the importance of giving people the space to tell their stories at the start of therapy. Not all will accept this invitation. As with Richard, some will offer only snippets of information until they feel more comfortable.]

Laura: It was a condition of his probation.

Bob: Do you think that was her way of getting you to come, or would you have come on your own if she would have just recommended it?

Richard: If I didn't have to, I wouldn't be here.

Laura: She had to make him come . . . 'cause he wouldn't have come.

BOB: I can understand that you wouldn't have come without her telling you to . . . but I'm glad you're here. Did she say to you what she thinks needs to happen here?

RICHARD: I don't remember.

LAURA: Yes you do . . . she said you need to find some ways to handle your anger better.

BOB: Can you be more specific about that? What does he do when he's angry?

[I'm looking for an action description here.]

LAURA: He gets mad, then there's hell to pay 'cause he won't listen. He just takes off and does what he pleases.

BOB: Takes off and leaves?

LAURA: Yeah, he goes wherever he wants and comes home when he feels like it.

BOB (TO RICHARD): What about that? Would you add or change anything about that?

RICHARD: I don't know.

BOB: OK, he gets angry and takes off sometimes . . . what else might have led your juvenile officer to send you here?

[I said that "sometimes" he takes off, suggesting that he doesn't do it every time.]

RICHARD: 'Cause I was with some friends and we got caught after curfew. It wasn't any big deal . . . she's just always on my case about something.

BOB: So, because sometimes she's had to lay down the law with you, it's felt like she's hassling you. How many times were you out after curfew?

[When people use statements that are generalized and closed down, we want to find small, subtle ways of opening up possibilities. There are several ways to do this. In this instance, I slightly modified Richard's statement in three ways. First, I used "sometimes" instead of "always." Next, I changed the tense to the past. Thus, she is not currently on his case, but has done so previously. Last, I translated his statement of what was happening into a perception by saying, "You feel like." It is important to acknowledge and validate without closing down the possibilities for change; however, the therapist must balance the two because too much of either can also close down avenues of change.]

RICHARD: Once.

LAURA: Well, it was two times really . . . but you leave all the time . . . .

RICHARD (ANGRILY): . . . No I don't! One time, mom!

LAURA: He has selective memory. One time that I reported it, but two times altogether, at least . . . and a few other times he left and came back right after curfew.

BOB: OK, two times, possibly more, but only one time it was actually reported, and a few where he left and then came back soon after.

LAURA: Right.

BOB: How come you don't take off every time you get angry?

RICHARD: I just don't.

BOB: All right. Maybe that will become clearer later. So what else?

[Richard declined my invitation to explore times when he doesn't take off. I respect that and don't push. I may or may not come back to it later.]

LAURA: He was bombing out at school . . . bad grades . . . and a fight.

BOB: With . . .

RICHARD: . . . I got suspended. It's a joke. The school's a joke, the teachers are a joke . . . they don't like me.

BOB: So far school's been like a joke for you.

[Here's another example of a subtle linguistic shift. I presupposed the possibility of finding future solutions by saying "so far."]

RICHARD: I can't help it if they don't like me, it's stupid anyway.

BOB: So, I'm a bit unclear here. You're on probation because of some things, like, school for one. Then there's the curfew violation. It sounds like you're acquainted with trouble, but it's strange to me that you earned probation for what you've told me so far. What am I missing . . . the fight?

[There are two considerations at this juncture. First, I could have gone to the referral to get all of the information I needed. However, I am more interested in the youth's "story" about the situation. Second, as previously discussed, a possibility-oriented approach taps into those elements of any theory that may be helpful. Here, I borrowed a page from narrative theory and externalized "trouble" in an effort to establish a relationship between Richard and his problem. Again, we're interested in how ideas can coexist.]

RICHARD: It's not that bad . . . but she [the DJO] got mad at me because I didn't go to school for a while, then when I went back I got in a fight.

BOB: How much school did you miss?

RICHARD: I can't remember.

LAURA: Over three months.

BOB: And the fight?

RICHARD: This kid punched me so I fought back.

[This was later confirmed by his juvenile officer. Both teenagers were charged with assault.]

BOB: OK, and as far as you can tell, missing school and the fight were what landed you on probation?

RICHARD: Yeah.

BOB: OK. Anything else?

RICHARD: No, that's it.

BOB (LOOK TO THE MOTHER): Anything you'd like to add, change?

[To strive for consensus, I give each person the opportunity to cocreate and shape the story.]

LAURA: Not really. That's about it, but he'd better watch it because he's already been given too many chances . . . she's [DJO] told him she's not messing around . . . she's reached the end with him.

BOB: She means business and probably won't let it go on much longer . . . she's at the end. *(to Richard)* All right, so what do you think about your situation?

RICHARD: It sucks!

BOB: What about it sucks?

RICHARD: I can't do anything because of probation. I have to call her every Tuesday and be in early . . . it sucks. She has to know everything . . . it's none of her business.

BOB: It seems like you can't do anything . . . you've got more restrictions than before.

RICHARD: Yeah. *(in a mocking tone)* Oh boy, I get to stay home with my family!

LAURA: Wow! What a concept! Have you actually ever tried it?

RICHARD: No, and I don't plan to!

BOB: I'm curious, though, because you've encountered rules before; how are these rules different than any others?

RICHARD: Because if I break them she already told me I'm going to DYS.

[DYS is the Missouri Division of Youth Services.]

BOB: OK, but they still are just rules and you've risked stiff consequences before . . . .

RICHARD: . . . I don't want to be locked up.

BOB: So what is it about you that you've decided that you don't want to be locked up?

[By asking this type of question, Richard finds himself in a situation of defining the parameters of who he is. These types of questions are sometimes tough for youth to answer, so if they don't work, I just move on.]

RICHARD: I couldn't do anything then!

BOB: Well, your lifestyle would definitely change, but how do you know that being locked up isn't for you?

RICHARD: I'm not a criminal! I just did some things I shouldn't.

[Here is part of Richard's story about himself. He knows what he is not—"a criminal."]

BOB: OK. I just want to check some things out with you so that I'm clear on what we're doing here. Tell me if I'm off base here, OK? So

Richard, your DJO sent you here because she thought you needed to learn to manage your anger better. And sometimes in the past when you've been angry you've taken off. Laura, you mentioned several things that are of concern to you like his poor grades, being in a fight, running away, and breaking curfew. And those are the things that landed him on probation. And Richard, I'm hearing from you that you don't want to get locked up. It seems like everyone wants the same thing. Your DJO doesn't want to have you locked up but she will if she has to. Laura, you don't want to see Richard placed in residential treatment but you're also frustrated with his behavior. Richard, you don't want to be locked up because you don't see yourself as a criminal and that would take you away from your family and friends. So we're all talking about finding ways that Richard can change his behavior so that he doesn't get locked up? Is that right?

[I offer a summary of what I think has transpired this far. The reason for this is: I want to gain a focus on where we're going. This enables me to construct a mutual goal of helping Richard to change his behavior so that he will not be placed residentially. If I'm off base, the family will correct me and we can modify the goal.]

Laura: That's exactly right.

Bob: Richard?

Richard: Yep. I don't want to be locked up.

Bob: OK. So let's suppose that we jumped ahead three or four months into the future, and things were going the way you'd like. And we were able to catch it on videotape. If I were to watch it, how would I know things were better? What would I see happening?

[I want to get an idea of what things will look like when they're better, so I ask for an action description of things in the future.]

Laura: He wouldn't be taking off and doing all that stuff at school.

Bob: What would he be doing instead?

[I'm searching for what he will be doing as opposed to what he won't be doing.]

Laura: He'd handle his anger better and not take off. And his grades would be better and he wouldn't be fighting with other kids.

Bob: Great. And maybe he's already moving that way or he soon will be—I'm not sure. But what will be a sign that he's moving in that direction?

[Sometimes, change begins before therapy does. I merely want to suggest that that's a possibility. If it hasn't begun, I'm presupposing that it will at some time in the near future.]

Laura: If he didn't run away for a week and did some schoolwork.

Bob: When was the last time that you caught him doing schoolwork?

[I use a slight play on words here, suggesting that she might "catch" her son doing something good.]

Laura: He actually did a book report last week.

Bob: Really? What was it on?

Richard: How baseball players make it to the major leagues.

Bob: That's great. What did you learn?

Richard: Only a few players are good enough to make it.

Bob: Yeah, it's a very competitive process. How did you manage to get the report done?

Richard: I was interested in it, so it was easy.

Bob: OK, you were interested and that made it easier for you, but you could have blown it off because it was work.

Richard: I know, but I'm tired of people thinking bad about me.

Bob: Do you think that some people have the wrong idea about you?

Richard: Yeah, they don't know me . . . they just think they do.

Bob: Who?

Richard: My mom, my teachers, my DJO . . . .

Bob: . . . they have ideas about you, don't they?

Richard: They don't know what I'm about . . . I'm not bad. I just get in trouble sometimes.

Bob: Are they having a hard time seeing what you're all about and what you stand for?

Richard: Sometimes.

BOB: Sometimes?

RICHARD: Sometimes it's cool and they know it is.

BOB: How do they know it's cool?

RICHARD: 'Cause I don't always do bad things.

BOB: So there's been times that things are cool and they get to see what you're really about.

RICHARD: Yeah.

BOB: And when it's cool, that's one thing; and other times, trouble interferes and people don't know what's up.

RICHARD: Yeah.

BOB: So how has trouble wedged its way into your life so that people don't always know what's up . . . what you're really about?

[I stick with the externalization here, but not in a typical narrative way because I move in and out of that metaphorical frame as the dialogue evolves.]

RICHARD: I just . . . sometimes I do things I shouldn't.

BOB: How often does that kind of thing happen with you?

[Throughout the therapy, I continue to attend to patterns including intensity, frequency, and duration.]

RICHARD: Sometimes.

BOB: And sometimes it doesn't?

RICHARD: A lot of times I don't get into trouble.

BOB: OK, so help me out here. What percentage of the time would you say you handle trouble well, and what percentage of the time does trouble interfere and get the upper hand?

RICHARD: About 80% of the time I do good.

[Percentage questions can be helpful in quantifying behaviors.]

BOB: 80%? OK. Laura, what do you think?

LAURA: 80% is probably right, but it only takes a bad decision here or there and things get out of hand.

BOB: Right, one poor decision, even if a person is batting .900, can be enough if the decision is a poor enough one. So how often do the really poor decisions happen, versus those that still aren't good, but they're tolerable and not damaging or illegal?

Laura: Only once in a while . . . like once every four or five months.

Bob: What would be an example of a really poor decision?

Laura: Like, stealing or getting arrested or suspended. He knows what I can't tolerate.

Bob: OK, so he's clear on that. *(to Richard)* Right?

[I want to invite Richard to be responsible and accountable. One way to do this is by making sure he is clear on what is expected of him.]

Richard: Yeah.

Bob: So if he was to stay at 80%, and maybe even move toward 85%, and not have any really poor decisions, would you say that he's moving in the right direction?

[Suggestions of small, incremental change are often more attainable. Sometimes, expectations for larger change can be too overwhelming.]

Laura: Definitely. That's all I'm asking for.

Bob: OK. Richard, I'm curious, what do you do instead . . . that sometimes you get the upper hand with trouble when you're about to give in and make a poor decision?

Richard: I just don't do it.

Bob: Do you think it's because you're getting older and more mature? Or, you just don't think it's right for you? Or, you're worried about hurting others . . . like your family or girlfriend, or maybe something else . . . ?

[As discussed, youth are great at responding with, "I don't know." (And usually they really don't know!) When this happens, we can use multiple-choice responses for two particular reasons. First, they may choose one that fits for them, or say "None of the above" and give an alternative response. Either way, multiple-choice questions can generate further information. Second, just by mentioning some possibilities and using speculation, the youth can attribute some part of the better decision making to something that is difficult to deny. That is, would youth say they are *not* becoming more responsible? Or deny that they don't want to hurt people close to them?]

RICHARD: . . . yeah, probably those things.

BOB: So it's probably those things and maybe some other things too. That may become clearer to you sooner or later. What do you think might begin to help others see more of what you're really about and less of trouble?

[I typically leave suggestions for youth and they can take or leave them. My interpretations are just that; they're mine. I am interested in youth developing their own conclusions about how and why they may be changing. So I leave it open by suggesting that things may become clearer at some point.]

RICHARD: I don't know because my DJO thinks I'm just gonna keep screwing up.

BOB: You think she has that idea about you. OK. I once worked with a teenager who swore up and down that his teachers had it in for him. No matter what, he was going to get the shaft. He finally decided that the only thing he could do was to show others what he was about . . . because people were unsure . . . one minute he was cool and another he was in trouble. His teachers had the idea about him that he was a troublemaker and wasn't going to do any work. But every once in a while he would hand in an assignment and that was confusing to them. So, for one week, he handed in all of his assignments and didn't cause any trouble. He was shocked when one of his teachers smiled at him in the hallway. Then another pulled him aside and asked him if he wanted help catching up. That was a weird thing, because his teachers may have had the idea about him that he was a troublemaker and not willing to work in school, but when he did show them what he was about, their stories about him changed. Then, one day he didn't hand in his assignment for a class because he was really sick, and his teacher said, "OK." She believed him. The teacher's story about him changed. She expected him to hand in his homework and when he didn't she knew there was a good reason. I wonder what it might be like for you if some of the people in your life began to change their stories about you . . . and maybe they already are changing or have changed. I'm not sure. But you mentioned something a minute ago that I'm curious about. You said that you hadn't been doing too good at school. I heard about you doing the book report. What else is different now?

[Stories help to normalize things and offer possible solutions. I often tell one and then shift to a question about something else at the end. Stories don't require verbal responses from adolescents. They can be offered to youth as a vehicle to generate new meanings that may be helpful to them.]

Laura: Actually, his grades have improved.

Bob: Really? Like from what to what?

Richard: From Fs to Ds . . . and one C.

Bob: How do you explain that?

Richard: I just did it.

Bob: How did you get yourself to do it, because you could have found many reasons not to?

Richard: I just started to try, I guess.

Laura: He's actually very smart . . . he's had good grades before. He just doesn't do the work.

Bob: So it doesn't seem to be about ability. It's more about putting the pencil to the paper . . . doing it?

Laura: Yeah.

Bob: You know, you never really forget what it's like to get good grades. You might have to go back a few years, I'm not sure, but there's very different feelings that go with good grades than go with bad grades. Do you know what I mean?

[This is an assumption that I share with many others; that the mind stores experience that can be retrieved. In this case, the evocation of positive past experiences and associated feelings can be a nice building block.]

Richard: Yeah.

Bob: What do good grades feel like to you?

[There seems to be an unhelpful assumption, an unwritten rule, suggesting that feeling-oriented questions have no place in solution-based therapies. Thus, this type of question is often not used because it asks clients to explore the domain of experience. In possibility therapy, there are multiple pathways for creating change.]

RICHARD: Good.

BOB: OK. Anything else?

RICHARD: Not really.

BOB (TO THE MOTHER): What's that been like for you, that his grades have been improving?

LAURA: It's great. I know he can do it.

BOB: I wonder how your teachers' stories about you are changing. I also wonder what you'll be doing in between this session and the next, to convince people that home is the place for you.

SESSION TWO

[The elapsed time between sessions was two weeks. I usually will see youth one week after the initial session; then, depending on the circumstances, begin to spread them out over time. On this occasion, I had been traveling the prior week and was not able to see Richard and Laura until two weeks later.]

BOB: What's happening?

RICHARD: Not much. But I haven't been in trouble.

BOB: Really? You haven't been in what kind of trouble?

RICHARD: Any trouble.

LAURA: He really hasn't. But he's done that before.

BOB: Done what before . . . gone a while without giving in to trouble?

LAURA: Yeah. He can go for a few weeks and then all hell breaks loose.

RICHARD (ANGRILY TOWARD MOTHER): How do you know? Sometimes it doesn't!

LAURA: Richard!

BOB: So you didn't give in to trouble for the last two weeks, and how long did you go before we first met?

RICHARD: I've done OK since I went to court.

LAURA: Richard . . . you went to court on the third and skipped school on the ninth! We came here on the eleventh . . . so just two days before we came.

BOB: OK, so two weeks and two days.

LAURA: Right.

BOB (TO RICHARD): Is that right?

RICHARD: I guess.

BOB: So, there's this thing that happens in sports. Players often have these things called streaks and slumps. Ever hear of them?

RICHARD: Yeah, like when a player gets "hot."

BOB: Right, that's a streak. Now, when a player is on a streak, everything seems to fall in place. For a baseball player, it might be that he hits balls that would normally be routine outs and they somehow find the holes in the defense and he gets on base. The player gets breaks. You have to play well but you also need breaks to have a streak. A slump happens when a player doesn't get many breaks, and balls that are hit hard end up being right at somebody. It's very frustrating. Every player has streaks and slumps. But if you watch closely, most of the time you'll see that the players that work hard day after day, and are dedicated, usually just have bad games here and there. Their slumps are very brief. Michael Jordan has games where he's off, but it doesn't last. Same with Ron Gant. And if they do hit a brief slump, they work hard to get back on track, and the rest of their game doesn't necessarily suffer. *(to Richard)* What do you think it will take for you not to have long slumps and extend the streaks?

[Richard is a big sports fan, as am I. So I take every opportunity to use sports-associated metaphors and stories. Michael Jordan needs no introduction. Ron Gant is an outfielder for the St. Louis Cardinals.]

RICHARD: *(silence)*

LAURA: He just needs to make up his mind . . . so many people are willing to help him, but he's got to make an effort too.

BOB: Right. Players have a manager and all sorts of coaches to help out—and other players too; but they can't do the work for the player.

LAURA: Right . . . they just help the player.

BOB: Richard, do you experience streaks and slumps?

RICHARD: I'm on a streak right now!

BOB: That's right . . . two weeks and two days. How do you extend a streak? What would Grant Fuhr do?

[Grant Fuhr is a goaltender for the St. Louis Blues Hockey Club.]

RICHARD: He'd stay focused.

BOB: How would he do that?

RICHARD: Just concentrate and not let things bother him, I guess.

BOB: What might bother a goalie who's on a streak?

RICHARD: Bad goals.

BOB: So a bad goal or so might throw off a goalie . . . get him off his game.

RICHARD: Right.

BOB: But by staying focused, and maybe continuing to work hard, he can continue to improve his game?

RICHARD: Yeah.

BOB: And now you've got a streak of your own. What will you be doing to keep it going?

RICHARD: It's not that hard. I just have to try hard.

BOB: As you are trying hard and continuing your streak, what will you be doing?

RICHARD: Not doing stupid things.

BOB: What's an example of not doing something stupid?

RICHARD: This kid at school wanted me to fight. He was saying stuff, but I didn't.

Bob: Wow! So there's this kid at school and he's like, "Let's go." And you're like, "Not this time, that's not for me."

Richard: I could have kicked his ass . . . but I just blew out and went home.

Bob: So trouble was lingering by, but you didn't give in.

Richard: Yeah . . .

Bob: . . . and the streak goes on. *(to the mother)* And he's had some streaks before, and you've been wondering how long he's going to go this time. (The mother nods "Yes.") How long do you think he will need to go before people start to wonder, "Hey, maybe he's got the upper hand with trouble?"

Laura: I'd like to see him go two months. That would be a good start.

Bob: It's funny how things can become automatic after a while. *(to Richard)* When you were younger, you didn't have to think about whether or not you were going to go to school. You just did it. You woke up, got dressed, ate breakfast, and went to school. It was routine and automatic. Now, maybe that's becoming automatic again for you. I don't know. I wonder how long it will be before you automatically stand up to trouble. Or, maybe it's already beginning to happen. I don't know. What I'm curious about is: how have others reacted to you being at school more regularly, getting better grades, not fighting, not being in trouble?

[This is another example of evoking a previous experience so that youth can see an event such as getting up each day as an already existing ability. The idea of automaticity can also be helpful with youth. Getting up doesn't have to be an ordeal; it can be a routine thing.]

Richard: Huh?

Bob: Are they surprised? Did they know you could do it if you put your mind to it? Are they doubting whether you will keep it up?

Richard: My teachers are surprised. They still think I'm gonna mess up . . . they don't know.

Bob: OK . . .

RICHARD: . . . they're just waiting for me to mess up.

BOB: From what you've encountered, it seems like they're waiting for you to mess up. Maybe they're skeptical, waiting to see if you hit a slump.

[Skepticism is understandably abundant with youth who are in situations similar to Richard's. Further, because Richard has a history of finding trouble, his DJO would likely not be surprised if he did so again. Still, it's equally unlikely that she is "waiting" for him to "mess up." That is a statement that I feel is unhelpful, so I note it as a perception by using the word "seems."]

RICHARD: They're going to be waiting a long time.

SESSION THREE

[The elapsed time between sessions two and three was two weeks.]

BOB: Where are we at with things?

RICHARD: No trouble!

BOB: Huh?

RICHARD: I haven't been in any trouble . . . ask my mom.

BOB: Well?

LAURA: He's right. We just passed a month, and so far so good. I don't think his juvenile officer is convinced, though.

BOB: Yeah, "Just the facts, ma'am." And it makes sense that people are skeptical. You yourself said that two months would be a good measure. *(looks to Richard)* So, your DJO needs to be convinced that what is happening isn't a fluke. Hank Aaron became the all-time home run leader by hitting home runs for 20-plus seasons, but other players have had one good season, then were given big contracts and fell flat. She wants to be sure about you over time, otherwise it will come back to haunt her. What will you continue doing to convince her otherwise . . . so that she is less skeptical and more convinced that you are going to do well over time?

[My experience with DJOs has been that, when a youth does well over time, they are more than willing to make concessions. However, they want proof, and often that translates to good behavior over extended periods of time. Hank Aaron is a baseball legend and Major League Baseball's all-time home run leader.]

RICHARD: Just to keep doing what I'm doing . . . but she doesn't tell me . . . so how should I know?

BOB: My guess is she would say you've got to watch your anger.

[This is a reorientation to part of the initial goal of therapy and why he was originally referred.]

RICHARD: I've been mad but I haven't taken off.

BOB: And how will you be continuing to do that?

RICHARD: I just go to my room and do something else.

BOB: Can you think of anything that might come up that might be a hurdle for you?

RICHARD: Not really.

BOB: OK. What else will you be doing to convince her and your mother that home is where you ought to be?

RICHARD: I don't know what else.

BOB: Have you seen your contract? Your terms of probation?

RICHARD: Yeah.

BOB: What does it say you should do?

RICHARD: Just stay out of trouble. Oh yeah, I have to call her on Tuesdays, check in . . . and be in by 8:30 *(in the evening)*. I can't stay at my friend's unless I ask her. There's too many rules.

BOB: There are a lot of rules, and some are tougher than others, and that's what I'm curious about. How have you managed to stay on course? By doing those things . . . and maybe some other things too?

[I want to be sure and explore what else he has been doing that might be positive, not just the conditions of his probation. It's also a cue to his mother to notice other changes.]

RICHARD: Yeah, but I don't like it.

BOB: And that's what amazes me because you have reasons that you could've ditched your probation, but you have continued to play your game and keep the streak alive. I keep wondering about that.

RICHARD: It's not that hard. I just don't like it.

BOB: OK, so is it like you're just continuing to do what you do and maybe it's more automatic now?

RICHARD: Yeah, I don't have to really think too much about it.

BOB: Laura, what have you noticed?

LAURA: You know, he's done great with his probation. He goes to school and does most of his work—not all of it . . . but most. I can see why it's frustrating for him because it's like there's no light at the end of the tunnel. He doesn't know where it ends and where it begins.

[During this session, the mother seemed to move more toward Richard's side and to become more of an advocate for him.]

BOB: Right, because just a few weeks ago he was close to being placed, and so it's hard to know where he stands. That's a tough situation to be in. You know, you probably already know this from the report you did in school, but there's a percentage of athletes, each year, that don't know whether or not they will make the team they are trying out for. And Olympic athletes sometimes have to wait years before they are able to compete at the level they want to. How do they keep their vision alive? They have a sense that someday it will happen, but sometimes it's hard to keep going because it seems so far away.

[I want to orient Richard toward his preferred future where he's no longer at risk of being placed and is off probation.]

LAURA: That's true.

BOB: How do you keep that vision alive, Richard? Of being off probation, of getting a driver's permit, or whatever you see in front of you?

RICHARD: I just have to keep going.

Bob: Every day that you move toward the future, the past becomes farther away. *(to Laura)* So where do you see things in relation to the goal of Richard improving his behavior and convincing people that he belongs at home?

[I want to keep an eye on the goals of therapy and stay clear on how we will know when things are better and therapy should end.]

Laura: I think we're getting there. In the back of my mind, I still wonder if he'll keep it up.

Bob: What might give you the sense that things will be OK? How will you know when he's out of the woods, knowing that there may be some ups and downs?

Laura: I really think time is the key here. He just has to continue doing what he's doing for a while longer.

Bob: That makes sense. So how long do you think things would need to go for you to be more comfortable about things?

Laura: I'm thinking that if he went another three or four weeks or so, I'd feel good about him being out of the woods.

SESSION FOUR

[I was out of town for much of the period in between sessions three and four. The elapsed time was four weeks.]

Bob: OK, so it's been around a month since we last met, and I have no idea what's happened during that time . . . so, who wants to fill me in?

Laura: Well, really, he's been OK. He hasn't been in any trouble . . . that I know of . . . .

Richard: . . . I haven't at all!

Bob: No trouble?

Richard: Nope!

Laura: We've had some small things at home, like Richard not taking out the trash, but to me, that falls into that area of things I can tolerate. It's the serious stuff, and the court stuff, that I get freaked about.

BOB: OK, you'd appreciate it if he'd do what he needs to do at home, but at the moment your focus is on the serious stuff. So, no further incidences with the court?

LAURA: That's right.

BOB: Richard, what have you been doing to stay on track?

RICHARD: I'm just doing my homework and it's not that hard.

BOB: What else have you been doing?

RICHARD: Just going by my probation even though I don't like it.

BOB: And that must take some real commitment from you—to do it when you don't like it.

RICHARD: Yeah.

BOB (TO LAURA): What's that like for you . . . to witness this?

LAURA: It's really nice. I know he cares.

BOB: It's like he's thinking of not just himself but others too.

LAURA: Exactly.

BOB: Richard, I'm a bit confused by all this because you've been continuing this streak. "Inquiring minds want to know," what's the story?

RICHARD: The story is . . . I just did it.

BOB: And what would the headline read? "Young whippersnapper continues streak!"

RICHARD (LAUGHTER FROM ALL): No . . . it would say, "Richard was right!"

BOB: Right about what?

RICHARD: I'm not getting in trouble, so I was right and they weren't.

BOB: They . . . ?

RICHARD: You know, my DJO . . . .

[Although he said, "they," he did not mention his mother or teachers this time. He later stated that he felt they were on his side.]

BOB: So you have gone for how long now?

RICHARD: I can't remember. I think two months.

LAURA: Yeah, it has been over two months.

BOB: Are you surprised?

LAURA: Yeah. I was waiting for the tidal wave to come and it hasn't.

BOB: There hasn't been any big disaster but you were feeling like, "When's it going to happen?"

LAURA: Right.

BOB: And now it seems different?

LAURA: It's very different. I'm not as worried as I was before.

BOB: You mentioned last time that if he went another three or four weeks you might feel more comfortable about things. Has that happened for you?

LAURA: It has. I guess I'll always have a twinge of worry, but now I don't worry about the school calling all the time or about the police calling. What a relief!

BOB: That's great to hear. *(to Richard)* You know, with all that's happened, I'm wondering, what have others noticed about you lately?

[As discussed, I think it is important to share change with a wider social context. It seems to make it more real and known, and anchor it in some way.]

RICHARD: My teachers have been cool.

BOB: How so?

RICHARD: They're leaving me alone. Mr. Young's been cool . . . he's off my case.

BOB: What does he know about you now that maybe he didn't before?

RICHARD: He knows I'm cool. I'm not gonna cause trouble.

BOB: He knows that about you? How did he discover that?

RICHARD: 'Cause I've been doing my work in class and he told me he'd help me catch up if I wanted, and I said, "OK."

Bob: It sounds to me like he's got a different story about you now.

Richard: He does.

SESSION FIVE

[Four more weeks elapsed before this final session.]

Richard: I met with my DJO!

Bob: What happened?

Richard: She told me if I keep it up I'll get off probation in April . . . if I don't mess up.

Bob: Really? How did that come about?

Richard: She just told me that since I was doing what I had to, she couldn't keep me on probation.

Bob: Wow!

Laura: Yeah, I talked with her and she said that she was looking to see if he could hold it together for an extended period of time . . . and he has, so she's going to let him off at six months instead of a year.

Bob: What do you think about that?

Laura: At first I was a little worried, but I think it's a good idea. He's done well for a long time. I know there's going to be some tough times, but I'm not worried about him doing what he did before.

Bob: What's different that you feel more confident about things now?

Laura: Just the fact that he hasn't been in any trouble for longer than any other time. I know he can do it.

Bob: OK, so the time factor . . . and maybe in the past you wondered if he really could do it for a long period of time, and now you've actually witnessed it. And maybe there will be some ups and downs, but not like the roller coaster ride before. So is there anything else that we should be talking about or doing, or do you feel like things are where they need to be?

Laura: I feel like he's done what he's needed to. He's stayed out of trouble.

Bob: Great! Richard, I have to wonder what this all means for you?

Richard: Just that I can start over again. I was at the end . . . now I'm at the beginning.

FOLLOW-UP

Richard's DJO contacted me about 10 weeks after the completion of the therapy to inform me that he was about to be released from probation. She stated that she was surprised at how "serious" he had become about his situation. Approximately seven months later, the mother called and related that Richard was doing well and had been working and playing organized sports. He had also won an award for sportsmanship on his team. She further remarked that the family was moving out of state. Recalling that previous moves had been difficult for the "family" (she did not single out Richard or any one family member), she asked, "Just in case of some rough waters, could you recommend someone that we could see who's near where we're moving?"

Approximately 15 months later, I heard from the mother. She stated that the family had to move back to town for "financial reasons." She offered, "Things are a bit tough money-wise, but we're doing OK. And Richard," she continued, "he's doing great! I just thought you'd want to know that."

CHAPTER NINE

A Return to Yourself

THERAPY THAT MAKES A DIFFERENCE

The big question is whether you are going to be able to say a hearty yes to your adventure.

—Joseph Campbell

I WAS DOING A *workshop at a local mental health center. A woman approached me during a break and said, "I usually sleep through these things because they're so boring and drab. I just go because I need the CEUs [continuing education credits]. But not only am I still awake, I'm feeling reenergized. Isn't that weird?" I responded, "I think that's wonderful. What do you suppose has reenergized you?" "It's just the fact that what you've been saying feels right to me. It resonates with every part of me and what I believe. I mean, you're teaching us ideas for working with kids, but it also feels to me like you're teaching us a way of dealing with life in general. I've needed that but didn't realize it until now."*

When I teach beginning master's level students, one of the first things I tell them is that the single most important therapeutic tool they have is themselves. Who they are and their personal uniqueness make a significant difference in the therapeutic milieu. I also stress the importance of finding a "fit" between what each student believes and the theory he or she chooses to practice. Colleagues have told me that they use similar approaches with their students. Despite this, for a variety of reasons, what actually happens with therapists in the "real" world is often far removed from these ideas.

In the real word, each day, many clinicians put on their respective "therapist hats," do their theories with clients, then go home and practice a different way of living. They live by two different theories—one for clients, and one for themselves and their families. A question arises: "Why do unto others what you don't believe to be true for yourself?" This incongruity is tough to fathom, and difficult to explain to students.

The interaction with the woman in the story at the beginning of this chapter reminded me that a possibility therapy approach does not rely on a technique or method. It's about a way of being with people—in and out of therapy. That is, both in and away from the office, we seek an improved quality of life for others and ourselves. The ideas in this book are meant to facilitate this process through respectful, collaborative, and realistic means. In essence, the ideas presented are useful in life, not just with clients.

Because a possibility therapy approach is a competency-based, change-oriented perspective, I believe such a focus can counter therapist burnout. Let's consider this. Adolescents and families are challenging and have driven many therapists to other types of clientele and even to other career paths. My wife, Christine, who works for a "gatekeeper" company for HMOs, has told me that, in certain parts of the United States, it's nearly impossible to find therapists who want to work with youth. When we combine the difficulty of working with adolescents and families with therapy approaches that only are pathology- or problem-focused, our job can become, over time, very disheartening and can yield a sense of hopelessness. Not surprisingly, this is what adolescents and family members experience—a sense of hopelessness that often leads them to therapy. For therapists, such feelings can lead to burnout.

As outlined throughout this book, a possibility therapy approach takes a different view. Instead of continually letting our theories tell us what can't be done, we focus on what's possible and what's changeable. We don't ignore the realities that adolescents and families face; we acknowledge and attend to them while simultaneously asking, "What else?" Such a view can breathe new life into cases and create optimism—not theories that drain therapists. The optimism, in turn, can counter therapist burnout.

COOKBOOKS ARE FOR COOKING:
THE RECIPE EXISTS WITHIN

It was late in the summer of 1997, and I was meeting with a 16-year-old female. Three months earlier, her father, mother, and stepmother had told me that she probably wouldn't come in because of a previous bad experience in therapy. It was now our last session, and I said to the teenager, "I had heard that you wouldn't come to see another therapist because you had a bad experience. So I wanted to thank you for coming and sticking it out. I hope it went OK this time." To this she replied, "This was much different than what I expected. You acted like a real person. All that other guy kept asking me was, 'If a miracle happened, what would your life be like?' I was, like, is that like a question in a book or something? Everything was about miracles or, 'On a scale of one to ten, what's your life like?' I hated that. It was like he didn't know any other questions."

It's a wonderful and exciting time to be a clinician. There is a wealth of great ideas that therapists have at their fingertips these days. The creative thinking and clinical work that are happening all over the world are definitely inspiring. At the same time, there's always a risk with the presentation of ideas, old or new. That is, in the teaching of approaches to therapy, sometimes we resort to using flow charts or diagrams. This is fine for teaching, but, as illustrated by the case above, that's not how therapy works.

If you were to read the works of many of the "masters" in the field of psychotherapy and then watch them do therapy, you would likely see something very interesting. That is, you wouldn't see them following a 1-2-3 sequence with clients, because each person has his or her own style or way of working with others, and it supercedes theory. Despite being experts on various models of therapy, the creators' and innovators' "default" positions typically are their ability to remain human with clients.

The possibility therapy approach offered in this book is not a "cookbook" model with a flow chart to guide the way. It is a client-focused approach. The ideas that I've presented are meant to facilitate adolescents' and family members' own abilities, within themselves or their social systems, to resolve their complaints. This requires that therapists remain human with clients. It is also my hope that the ideas offered in this book will serve as an adjunct to the ones that therapists already have that are respectful and effective, instead of becoming a replacement model.

WHO IS SMARTER: A PERSON OR A COMPUTER?

It has been said for years that computers are not as smart as people. Well, are they?

With today's technological advances, new computer software is being created at an alarming rate. Thus, we are feeding new and upgraded software into our computers on a regular basis. When we do this, our computers respond in a very interesting way. They tell us that they need to be rebooted so the system can be reconfigured. So we turn off our computers and then turn them on again. Interestingly, when this is done, our computers make the necessary changes and then proceed to operate as before. And what does the new software do? It enhances the functioning of our computer's hardware and previously existing software, therefore offering us more options.

As therapists, we go to workshops, read books and journals, watch videos, and learn new ideas and methods that are supposed to increase our effectiveness with clients. Essentially, we are upgrading our personal hardware too. But, unlike computers, we don't always reboot ourselves. We don't consider how the new learnings are going to work with our existing hardware. Instead, we just use our new ideas without reconfiguring our theories and beliefs.

So how did computers get so smart? We made them that way. Humans *are* smarter. But let's prove it as therapists. Here is my suggestion: Now that you have finished this book, make sure your default position is set to: "RETURN TO YOURSELF." Then, each time you learn something new, check with yourself and reconsider how what you've learned fits with who you are. You can't go wrong with who you are!

> *Learn your theories as well as you can, then put them aside when you touch the living miracle of the human soul.*
>
> —Carl Jung

REFERENCES

American Psychiatric Association. (1994). *Diagnostic and statistical manual of mental disorders* (4th ed.). Washington, DC: American Psychiatric Association.

Andersen, T. (Ed.). (1991). *The reflecting team: Dialogues and dialogues about the dialogues.* New York: Norton.

Anderson, H., & Goolishian, H. (1988). Human systems and linguistic systems: Evolving ideas about the implications for theory and practice. *Family Process, 27,* 371–393.

Anderson, H., & Goolishian, H. (1992). The client is the expert: A not-knowing approach to therapy. In S. McNamee & K. J. Gergen (Eds.), *Therapy as social construction: Inquiries in social construction* (pp. 25–39). Newbury Park, CA: Sage.

Bandler, R., & Grinder, J. (1975). *Patterns of the hypnotic techniques of Milton H. Erickson, M.D.* (Vol. 1). Capitola, CA: Meta.

Barker, P. (1985). *Using metaphors in psychotherapy.* New York: Brunner/Mazel.

Barker, P. (1996). *Psychotherapeutic metaphors: A guide to theory and practice.* New York: Brunner/Mazel.

Bateson, G. (1972). *Steps to an ecology of mind: A revolutionary approach to man's understanding of himself.* New York: Ballantine Books.

Berg, I. K. (1994). *Family based services: A solution-focused approach.* New York: Norton.

Berg, I. K., & de Shazer, S. (1993). Making numbers talk: Language in therapy. In S. Friedman (Ed.), *The new language of change: Constructive collaboration in psychotherapy* (pp. 5–24). New York: Guilford Press.

Berg, I. K., & Gallagher, D. (1991). Solution-focused brief treatment with adolescent substance abusers. In T. C. Todd & M. D. Selekman (Eds.), *Family therapy approaches with adolescent substance abusers* (pp. 93–111). Needham Heights, MA: Allyn & Bacon.

Berg, I. K., & Miller, S. D. (1992). *Working with the problem drinker: A solution-focused approach.* New York: Norton.

Berger, P. L., & Luckmann, T. (1966). *The social construction of reality: A treatise in the sociology of knowledge.* New York: Doubleday/Anchor Books.

Bertolino, R. (1998a). Rewriting youth stories: An activity with troubled youth. In L. Hecker & S. Deacon (Eds.), *The therapist's notebook: Homework, handouts, and activities for use in psychotherapy.* New York: Haworth Press.

Bertolino, R. (1998b). *An exploration of change: Investigating the experiences of psychotherapy trainees.* Unpublished doctoral dissertation, St. Louis University, St. Louis, MO.

Bertolino, R. (in press). *A teaching seminar with Bill O'Hanlon.* Bristol, PA: Brunner/Mazel.

Blumstein, A., Cohen, J., & Farrington, D. P. (1988). Criminal career research: Its value for criminology. *Criminology, 26,* 1–36.

Bobele, M., Gardner, G., & Biever, J. (1995). Supervision as social construction. *Journal of Systemic Therapies, 14*(2), 14–25.

Butterworth, E. (1993). Love: The one creative force. In J. Canfield & M. V. Hansen (Eds.), *Chicken soup for the soul: 101 stories to open the heart and rekindle the spirit* (pp. 3–4). Deerfield Beach, FL: Health Communications.

Carter, B., & McGoldrick, M. (Eds.). (1989). *The changing family life cycle: A framework for family therapy* (2nd ed.). Needham Heights, MA: Allyn & Bacon.

Chopra, D. (1989). *Quantum healing: Exploring the frontiers of mind/body medicine.* New York: Bantam Books.

Combs, G., & Freedman, J. (1990). *Symbol, story, and ceremony: Using metaphor in individual and family therapy.* New York: Norton.

Combs, G., & Freedman, J. (1994). Milton Erickson: Early postmodernist. In J. K. Zeig (Ed.), *Ericksonian methods: The essence of the story* (pp. 267–281). New York: Brunner/Mazel.

de Shazer, S. (1985). *Keys to solution in brief therapy.* New York: Norton.

de Shazer, S. (1988). *Clues: Investigating solutions in brief therapy.* New York: Norton.

de Shazer, S. (1991). *Putting difference to work.* New York: Norton.

de Shazer, S. (1994). *Words were originally magic.* New York: Norton.

Doherty, W. J., & Simmons, D. S. (1996). Clinical practice patterns of marriage and family therapy: A national survey of therapists and their clients. *Journal of Marital and Family Therapy, 22*(1), 9–26.

Dryfoos, J. G. (1990). *Adolescents at risk: Prevalence and prevention.* New York: Oxford University Press.

Duncan, B. L., Hubble, M. A., & Miller, S. D. (1997). *Psychotherapy with "impossible" cases: The efficient treatment of therapy veterans.* New York: Norton.

Durrant, M. (1993). *Residential treatment: A cooperative, competency-based approach to therapy and program design.* New York: Norton.

Efran, J., & Lukens, M. D. (1985). The world according to Humberto Maturana. *Family Therapy Networker, 9*(3), 23–25, 27–28, 72–75.

Elliott, D. S. (1994). Serious violent offenders: Onset, developmental course, and termination—The American Society of Criminology 1993 Presidential Address. *Criminology, 32,* 1–21.

Epston, D. (1997). I am a bear: Discovering discoveries. In C. Smith & D. Nylund (Eds.), *Narrative therapies with children and adolescents* (pp. 53–70). New York: Guilford Press.

Erickson, M. H. (1954). Special techniques of brief hypnotherapy. *Journal of Clinical and Experiential Hypnosis, 2,* 109–129.

Erickson, M. H. (1958/1980). Pediatric hypnotherapy. In E. L. Rossi (Ed.), *Innovative hypnotherapy: Vol. 4. The collected papers of Milton H. Erickson on hypnosis* (pp. 174–180). New York: Irvington.

Erickson, M. H. (1983). Utilizing unconscious processes in hypnosis. In E. L. Rossi, M. O. Ryan, & F. A. Sharp (Eds.), *Healing in hypnosis: Vol. 1. The seminars, workshops, and lectures of Milton H. Erickson* (pp. 61–98). New York: Irvington.

Eron, J. B., & Lund, T. W. (1996). *Narrative solutions in brief therapy.* New York: Guilford Press.

Evans, P., O'Connor, T., Meakes, E., Ricketts, P., Pickering, M. R., & Schuman, M. (1994). *Reflections from both sides of the mirror: A narrative approach.* Presented at the Ontario Association for Marriage and Family Therapy Conference, London, Ontario, Canada.

Federal Bureau of Investigation. (1996). *Single-session solutions. Crime in the United States 1995.* Washington, DC: Government Printing Office.

Fish, J. M. (1997). Paradox for complainants? Strategic thoughts about solution-focused therapy. *Journal of Systemic Therapies, 16*(3), 266–273.

Fisher, R., & Fisher, S. (1997). Are we justified in treating children with psychotropic drugs? In S. Fisher & R. Greenberg (Eds.), *From placebo to panacea: Putting drugs to the test.* New York: Wiley.

Frankl, V. (1959). *Man's search for meaning: An introduction to logotherapy.* New York: Touchstone.

Friedman, S. (1995). *The reflecting team in action: Collaborative practice in family therapy.* New York: Guilford Press.

Friedman, S. (1997). *Time-effective psychotherapy: Maximizing outcomes in an era of minimized resources.* Needham Heights, MA: Allyn & Bacon.

Furman, B., & Ahola, T. (1992). *Solution talk: Hosting therapeutic conversations.* New York: Norton.

Garfield, S. L. (1982). Eclecticism and integration in psychotherapy. *Behavior Therapy, 13,* 610–623.

Garfield, S. L. (1989). *The practice of brief psychotherapy.* New York: Pergamon Press.

Gentle Spaces News. (1995). Let there be peace. In J. Canfield & M. V. Hansen (Eds.), *A 2nd helping of chicken soup for the soul: 101 more stories to open the heart and rekindle the spirit* (pp. 297–298). Deerfield Beach, FL: Health Communications.

Gilligan, S. (1997a). *The courage to love: Principles and practices of self-relations psychotherapy.* New York: Norton.

Gilligan, S. (1997b). Living in a post-Ericksonian world. In W. J. Matthews & J. H. Edgette (Eds.), *Current thinking and research in brief therapy: Vol. 1. Solutions, strategies, and narratives* (pp. 1–23). New York: Norton.

Gilligan, S. G. (1990). Coevolution of primary process in brief therapy. In J. K. Zeig & S. G. Gilligan (Eds.), *Brief therapy: Myths, methods, and metaphors* (pp. 359–377). New York: Brunner/Mazel.

Gordon, D. (1978). *Therapeutic metaphors: Helping others through the looking glass.* Cupertino, CA: Meta.

Grinder, J., DeLozier, J., & Bandler, R. (1977). *Patterns of the hypnotic techniques of Milton H. Erickson, M.D.* (Vol. 2). Cupertino, CA: Meta.

Haley, J. (1973). *Uncommon therapy: The psychiatric techniques of Milton H. Erickson, M.D.* New York: Norton.

Haley, J. (Ed.). (1985). *Conversations with Milton H. Erickson, M.D.: Vol. 3. Changing children and families.* New York: Triangle Press.

Haley, J. (1987). *Problem-solving therapy* (2nd ed.). San Francisco: Jossey-Bass.

Haley, J. (1990). *Strategies of psychotherapy* (2nd ed.). Rockville, MD: Triangle Press.

Hashima, P., & Finkelhor, D. (1994). Violent victimization of youth versus adults in the National Crime Victimization Survey. In *Juvenile offenders and victims: 1997 update on violence* (pp. 4–5). Pittsburgh, PA: National Center for Juvenile Justice.

Henrink, R. (Ed.). (1980). *The psychotherapy handbook: The A to Z guide to more than 250 different therapies in use today.* New York: New American Library.

Herman, J. L. (1992). *Trauma and recovery: The aftermath of violence— from domestic abuse to political terror.* New York: Basic Books.

Higgins, G. O. (1994). *Resilient adults: Overcoming a cruel past.* San Francisco: Jossey-Bass.

Hoffman, L. (1990). Constructing realities: An art of lenses. *Family Process, 29,* 1–12.

Hoffman, L. (1995). Forward. In S. Friedman (Ed.), *The reflecting team in action: Collaborative practice in family therapy* (pp. ix–xiv). New York: Guilford Press.

Hoyt, M. F. (1994a). *Constructive therapies* (Vol. 1). New York: Guilford Press.

Hoyt, M. F. (1994b). Single-session solutions. In M. F. Hoyt (Ed.), *Constructive therapies* (Vol. 1, pp. 140–159). New York: Guilford Press.

Hoyt, M. F. (1996a). *Constructive therapies* (Vol. 2). New York: Guilford Press.

Hoyt, M. F. (1996b). Welcome to possibilityland: A conversation with Bill O'Hanlon. In M. F. Hoyt (Ed.), *Constructive therapies* (Vol. 2, pp. 87–123). New York: Guilford Press.

Hoyt, M. F. (1998). *The handbook of constructive therapies.* San Francisco: Jossey-Bass.

Hubble, M., & O'Hanlon, W. H. (1992). Theory countertransference. *Dulwich Centre Newsletter, 1,* 25–30.

Hudson, P. O., & O'Hanlon, W. H. (1991). *Rewriting love stories: Brief marital therapy.* New York: Norton.

James, W. (1984). The principles of psychology. In B. W. Wiltshire (Ed.), *William James: The essential writings* (pp. 44–161). Albany, NY: SUNY Press. (Original work published 1890)

Johnson, C. (1955). *Harold and the purple crayon.* New York: Harper-Collins.

Katz, A. M. (1991). Afterwords: Continuing the dialogue. In T. Anderson (Ed.), *The reflecting team: Dialogues and dialogues about the dialogues* (pp. 98–126). New York: Norton.

Kopp, R. R. (1995). *Metaphor therapy: Using client-generated metaphors in psychotherapy.* New York: Brunner/Mazel.

Koss, M. P., & Butcher, J. N. (1986). Research on brief psychotherapy. In A. E. Bergin & S. L. Garfield (Eds.), *Handbook of psychotherapy and behavior change* (3rd ed., pp. 627–663). New York: Wiley.

Kuehl, B. P. (1995). The solution-oriented genogram: A collaborative approach. *Journal of Marital and Family Therapy, 21*(3), 239–250.

Lambert, M. J. (1992). Implications of outcome research for psychotherapy integration. In J. C. Norcross & M. R. Goldfried (Eds.), *Handbook of psychotherapy integration* (pp. 94–129). New York: Basic Books.

Lankton, S. R., & Lankton, C. H. (1983). *The answer within: A clinical framework of Ericksonian hypnotherapy.* New York: Brunner/Mazel.

Lankton, S. R., & Lankton, C. H. (1986). *Enchantment and intervention in family therapy: Training in Ericksonian approaches.* New York: Brunner/Mazel.

Lawson, A., McElheran, N., & Slive, A. (1997). Single session walk-in therapy: A model for the 21st century. *Family Therapy News, 30*(4), 15, 25.

Lawson, D. (1994). Identifying pretreatment change. *Journal of Counseling and Development, 72,* 244–248.

Levitt, E. E. (1966). Psychotherapy research and the expectation-reality discrepancy. *Psychotherapy, 3,* 163–166.

Lipchik, E. (1988). Purposeful sequences for beginning the solution-focused interview. In E. Lipchik (Ed.), *Interviewing* (pp. 105–116). Rockville, MD: Aspen.

Madanes, C. (1981). *Strategic family therapy.* San Francisco: Jossey-Bass.

Madanes, C. (1984). *Behind the one-way mirror: Advances in the practice of strategic therapy.* San Francisco: Jossey-Bass.

McBride, J. (1997). *Steven Spielberg: A biography.* New York: Simon & Schuster.

McKeel, A. J. (1997). A clinician's guide to research on solution-focused brief therapy. In S. D. Miller, M. A. Hubble, & B. L. Duncan (Eds.),

Handbook of solution-focused brief therapy (pp. 251–271). San Francisco: Jossey-Bass.

McKeel, A. J., & Weiner-Davis, M. (1995). *Presuppositional questions and pretreatment change: A further analysis.* Unpublished manuscript.

Miller, S. D. (1994). The solution conspiracy: A mystery in three installments. *Journal of Systemic Therapies, 13*(1), 18–37.

Miller, S. D., Duncan, B. L., & Hubble, M. A. (1997). *Escape from Babel: Toward a unifying language for psychotherapy practice.* New York: Norton.

Miller, S. D., Hubble, M. A., & Duncan, B. L. (1995). No more bells and whistles. *Family Therapy Networker, 19*(2), 53–58, 62–63.

Mills, J. C., & Crowley, R. J. (1986). *Therapeutic metaphors for children and the child within.* New York: Brunner/Mazel.

Nylund, D., & Corsiglia, V. (1994). Attention to the deficits in attention-deficit disorder: Deconstructing the diagnosis and bringing forth children's special abilities. *Journal of Collaborative Therapies, 2*(2), 7–17.

Nylund, D., & Thomas, J. (1994). The economics of narrative. *Family Therapy Networker, 18*(6), 38–39.

O'Hanlon, B. (1982). Strategic pattern intervention: An integration of individual and family therapies based on the work of Milton H. Erickson. *Journal of Strategic and Systemic Therapies, 1*(4), 26–33.

O'Hanlon, B. (1994). The third wave. *Family Therapy Networker, 18*(6), 18–26, 28–29.

O'Hanlon, B. (1996a). Action, stories, and experience. In B. O'Hanlon (Ed.), *The handout book: Complete handouts from the workshops of Bill O'Hanlon* (p. 97). Omaha, NE: Possibility Press.

O'Hanlon, B. (1996b). Assessment questions. In B. O'Hanlon (Ed.), *The handout book: Complete handouts from the workshops of Bill O'Hanlon* (p. 3). Omaha, NE: Possibility Press.

O'Hanlon, B. (1996c). Acknowledgment and possibility in interviewing. In B. O'Hanlon (Ed.), *The handout book: Complete handouts from the workshops of Bill O'Hanlon* (p. 1). Omaha, NE: Possibility Press.

O'Hanlon, B. (1996d). Problematic stories. In B. O'Hanlon (Ed.), *The handout book: Complete handouts from the workshops of Bill O'Hanlon* (p. 38). Omaha, NE: Possibility Press.

O'Hanlon, B. (1996e). New possibilities for therapeutic conversations. In B. O'Hanlon (Ed.), *The handout book: Complete handouts from the workshops of Bill O'Hanlon* (p. 32). Omaha, NE: Possibility Press.

O'Hanlon, B., & Beadle, S. (1994). *A field guide to possibilityland: Possibility therapy methods.* Omaha, NE: Possibility Press.

O'Hanlon, B., & Bertolino, B. (1998). *Even from a broken web: Brief, respectful solution-oriented therapy for sexual abuse and trauma.* New York: Wiley.

O'Hanlon, B., & Wilk, J. (1987). *Shifting contexts: The generation of effective psychotherapy.* New York: Guilford Press.

O'Hanlon, S., & O'Hanlon, B. (1997). *Possibility therapy with families.* Unpublished manuscript.

O'Hanlon, W. (1998). An inclusive, collaborative, solution-based model of psychotherapy. In M. F. Hoyt (Ed.), *The handbook of constructive therapies.* San Francisco: Jossey-Bass.

O'Hanlon, W. H. (1987). *Taproots: Underlying principles of Milton Erickson's therapy and hypnosis.* New York: Norton.

O'Hanlon, W. H. (1990). A grand unified theory for brief therapy: Putting problems in context. In J. K. Zeig & S. G. Gilligan (Eds.), *Brief therapy: Myths, methods, and metaphors* (pp. 78–89). New York: Brunner/Mazel.

O'Hanlon, W. H. (1993). Possibility therapy: From iatrogenic injury to iatrogenic healing. In S. Gilligan & R. Price (Eds.), *Therapeutic conversations* (pp. 3–21). New York: Norton.

O'Hanlon, W. H., & Hexum, A. L. (1990). *An uncommon casebook: The complete clinical work of Milton H. Erickson, M.D.* New York: Norton.

O'Hanlon, W. H., & Weiner-Davis, M. (1989). *In search of solutions: A new direction in psychotherapy.* New York: Norton.

Parry, A., & Doan, R. E. (1994). *Story re-visions: Narrative therapy in the postmodern world.* New York: Guilford Press.

Penn, P., & Sheinberg, M. (1991). Stories and conversations. *Journal of Strategic and Systemic Therapies, 10,* 30–37.

Rogers, C. R. (1951). *Client-centered therapy.* Boston: Houghton Mifflin.

Rogers, C. R. (1961). *On becoming a person: A therapist's view of psychotherapy.* Boston: Houghton Mifflin.

Rosen, S. (1982). *My voice will go with you: The teaching tales of Milton H. Erickson.* New York: Norton.

Rosenbaum, R., Hoyt, M. F., & Talmon, M. (1990). The challenge of single-session therapies: Creating pivotal moments. In R. A. Wells & V. J. Giannetti (Eds.), *The handbook of brief psychotherapies* (pp. 165–189). San Francisco: Jossey-Bass.

Rowan, T., & O'Hanlon, B. (in press). *Solution-oriented therapy for chronic and severe mental illness.* New York: Wiley.

Rutter, M. (1987). Psychosocial resilience and protective mechanisms. 1987 meeting of the American Orthopsychiatric Association. *American Journal of Orthopsychiatry, 57*(3), 316–331.

Saleeby, D. (1994). Culture, theory, and narrative: The intersection of meanings in practice. *Social Work, 39*, 351–359.

Selekman, M. D. (1993). *Pathways to change: Brief therapy solutions with difficult adolescents.* New York: Guilford Press.

Selekman, M. D. (1997). *Solution-focused therapy with children: Harnessing family strengths for systemic change.* New York: Guilford Press.

Sells, S. P., Smith, T. E., Coe, M. J., Yoshioka, M., & Robbins, J. (1994). An ethnography of couple and therapist experiences in reflecting team practice. *Journal of Marital and Family Therapy, 20*(3), 247–266.

Selvini Palazzoli, M., Boscolo, L., Cecchin, G., & Prata, G. (1978). *Paradox and counterparadox.* New York: Jason Aronson.

Selvini Palazzoli, M., Boscolo, L., Cecchin, G., & Prata, G. (1980). Hypothesizing-circularity-neutrality. *Family Process, 19*, 73–85.

Smith, C. (1997). Introduction: Comparing traditional therapies with narrative approaches. In C. Smith & D. Nylund (Eds.), *Narrative therapies with children and adolescents* (pp. 1–52). New York: Guilford Press.

Smith, M. L., Glass, G. V., & Miller, T. I. (1980). *The benefits of psychotherapy.* Baltimore: Johns Hopkins University Press.

Smith, T. E., Yoshioka, M., & Winton, M. (1993). A qualitative understanding of reflecting teams I: Client perspectives. *Journal of Systemic Therapies, 12*(3), 28–43.

Snyder, H. N. (1996). The juvenile court and delinquency cases. *The Future of Children, 6*(3), 53–63.

Sowell, T. (1997, September 22). Dangerous labels. *Forbes,* 283.

Talmon, M. (1990). *Single session therapy: Maximizing the effect of the first (and often only) therapeutic encounter.* San Francisco: Jossey-Bass.

Thomas, B. (1994). *Walt Disney: An American original.* New York: Hyperion.

Tohn, S. L., & Oshlag, J. A. (1996). Solution-focused therapy with mandated clients: Cooperating with the uncooperative. In S. D. Miller, M. A. Hubble, & B. L. Duncan (Eds.), *Handbook of solution-focused brief therapy* (pp. 152–183). San Francisco: Jossey-Bass.

Wallas, L. (1985). *Stories for the third ear: Using hypnosis fables in psychotherapy.* New York: Norton.

Walter, J. L., & Peller, J. E. (1992). *Becoming solution-focused in brief therapy.* New York: Brunner/Mazel.

Watts, A. (1966). *The book: On the taboo against knowing who you are.* New York: Pantheon Books.

Weil, A. (1995). *Spontaneous healing: How to discover and enhance your body's natural ability to maintain and heal itself.* New York: Knopf.

Weiner-Davis, M., de Shazer, S., & Gingerich, W. J. (1987). Using pretreatment change to construct a therapeutic solution: An exploratory study. *Journal of Marital and Family Therapy, 13,* 359–363.

White, M. (1995). *Re-authoring lives: Interviews and essays.* Adelaide, South Australia: Dulwich Centre.

White, M., & Epston, D. (1990). *Narrative means to therapeutic ends.* New York: Norton.

Wolin, S. J., & Wolin, S. (1993). *The resilient self: How survivors of troubled families rise above adversity.* New York: Villard Books.

Zeig, J. K. (Ed.). (1980). *A teaching seminar with Milton H. Erickson.* New York: Brunner/Mazel.

Zimmerman, J., & Dickerson, V. (1996). *If problems talked: Narrative therapy in action.* New York: Guilford Press.

INDEX